DC COMICS

BATGIRL™

NEW HERO OF THE NIGHT

TM

By Matthew K. Manning

Illustrated by Patrick Spaziante

SCHOLASTIC INC.

All rights reserved. Published by Scholastic Inc., *Publishers since 1920*.
SCHOLASTIC and associated logos are trademarks and/or registered trademarks of Scholastic Inc.

ISBN 978-1-338-11741-7

10 9 8 7 6 5 4 3 2 1   17 18 19 20 21

Printed in the U.S.A.   40

First printing 2017

Book design by Rick DeMonico

CONTENTS

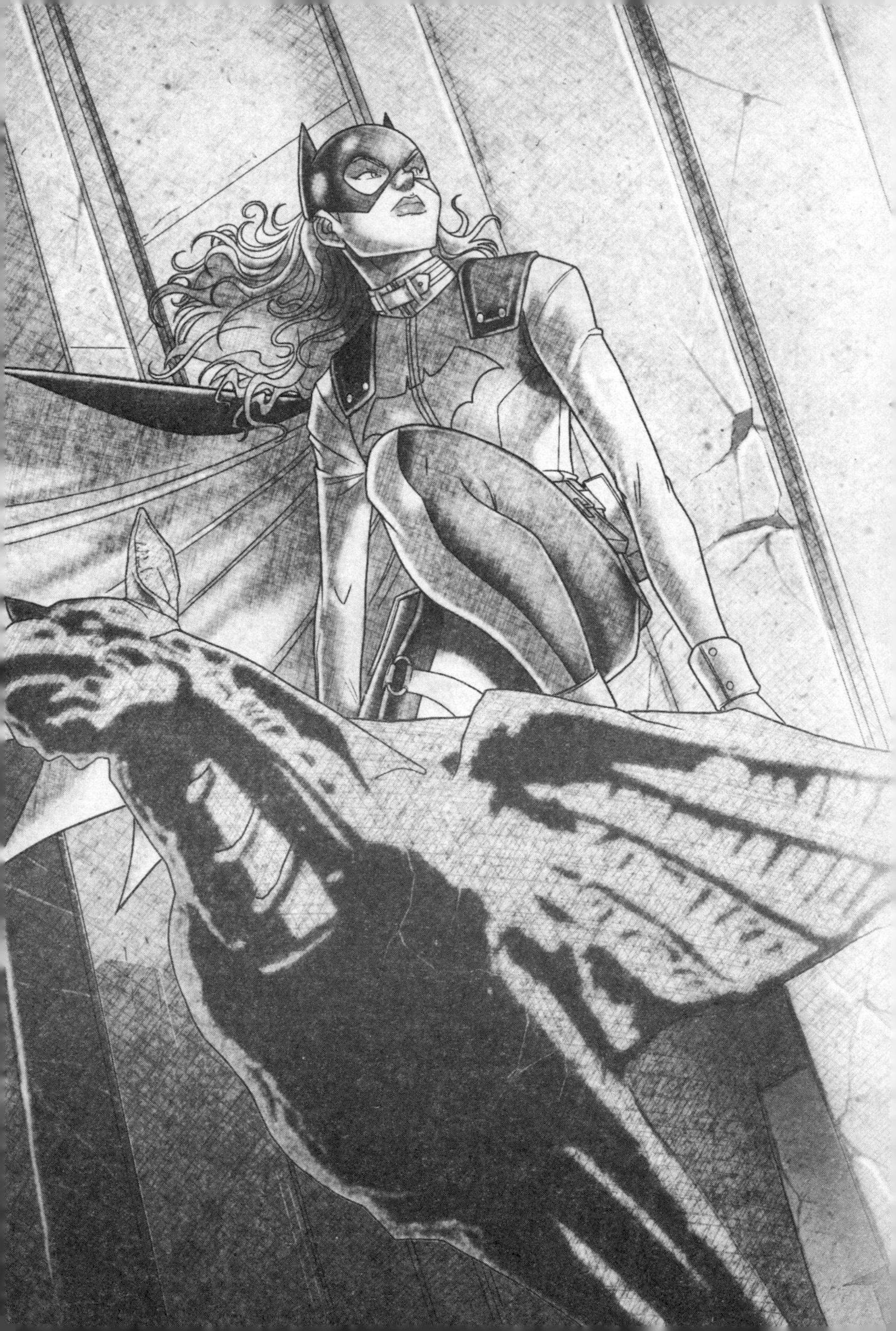

Foreword
by Batgirl

My name is Barbara Gordon, and I remember everything. I know how that sounds, but it's not an exaggeration. I was born with an eidetic memory, more commonly called a photographic memory. Everything I've ever studied, read, or even glanced at all stays with me. That comes in handy to me as a college student—but it's even more helpful during my night job. Because when the sun goes down, I stop being Barbara Gordon. I slip on a cowl and a cape and become the hero of the Gotham City borough of Burnside. Every night, I become Batgirl.

You've probably heard of my father: Gotham City's famous hero cop, Commissioner James Gordon. Having been raised by one of the few honest police officers in Gotham City, I've learned not to settle. My dad taught me that I don't have to accept things the way they are. Instead, I learned that it's my job to get out there and make the world just a little better than how I found it. He probably didn't mean for me to put on a pair of pointy ears and jump over rooftops hunting for criminals, but in my defense, he never outright told me *not* to do that, either. Honestly, if we're going to blame anyone for my dangerous late-night activities, it really should be my dad. If he didn't want me to join Batman's war on crime, he should have been more specific during our father-daughter chats.

Becoming Batgirl didn't just happen overnight. As it turned out, I'd been training for a life of fighting crime ever since I made my dad take me to my first judo lesson. Ever since I discovered the sheer

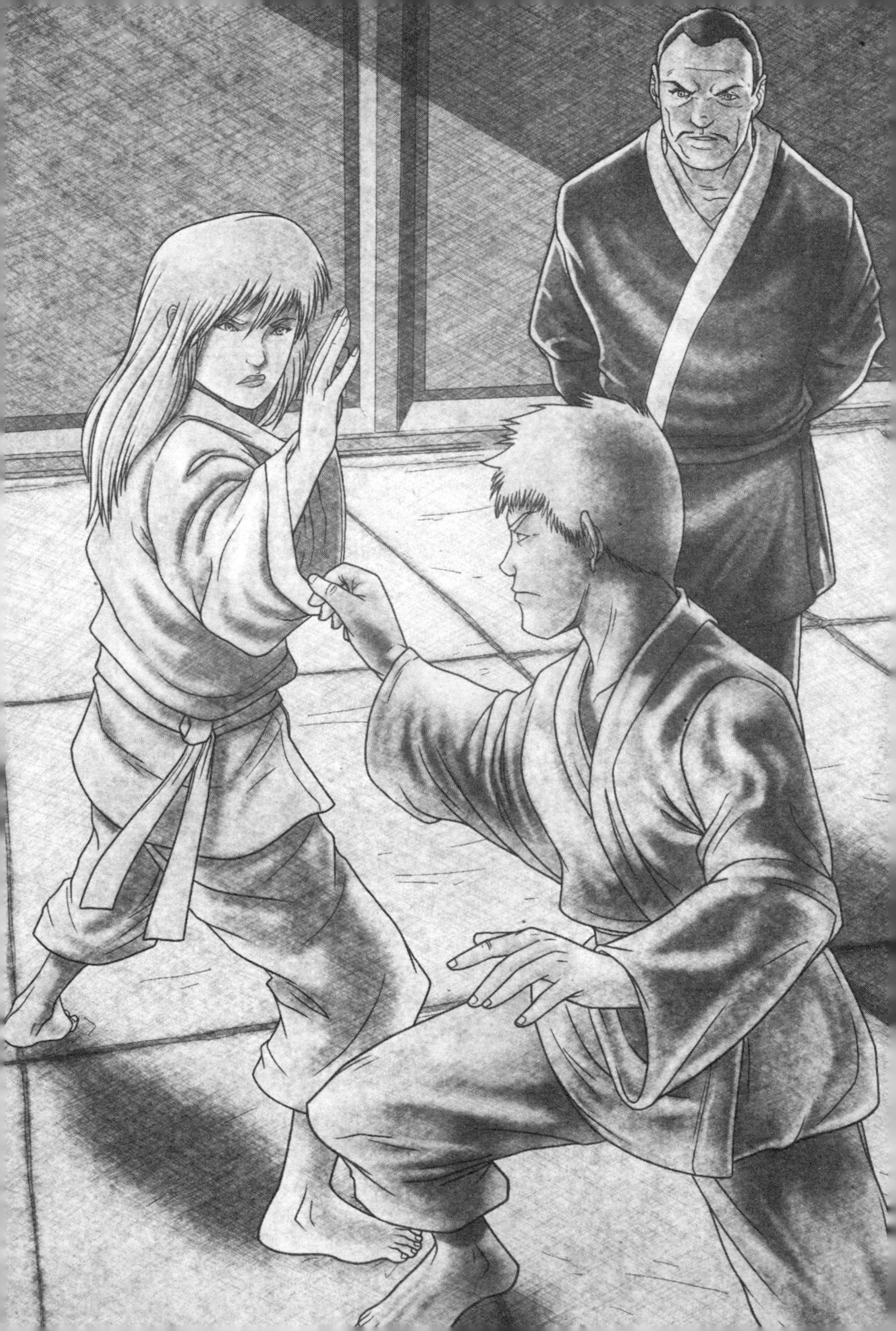

joy of gymnastics or cracked open my first book on criminology, I was developing skills that would help me later on in ways I never expected. When I approach a new fighting art or study a new language, I don't stop until I can do it perfectly. I'm not done until my skills match what I've studied and committed to memory.

When I first met the man called Batman, I had never seen a human move the way he did. He was dark and imposing, yet everything he said and everything he did was precise. Here was a man so good at fighting crime that my father realized a need for a person like him in a town as corrupt as Gotham City. Here was someone I could learn from. He had abilities that would take decades to match, if matching him was even possible.

It took time, training, and hard work, but Batman grew to accept me as one of his "soldiers." I went from being someone who desperately wanted his approval to someone who wanted to go into the world and do things my way. I'm no longer the little girl imitating her hero father. I'm no longer the teenager copying Batman's every move. Today, I'm the hero of Burnside and a founder of the Super Hero team called the Birds of Prey. But I'll always remember where I came from—because I'm Batgirl, and I remember everything.

Friends, Foes, and Family

Batgirl

Batgirl fights for justice in her own way, opting for wit over grit. A talented martial artist, computer expert, and detective, she has become the protector of the Gotham City borough of Burnside and a hero celebrated throughout the world.

Batman

Also known as the Dark Knight, or, by day, Bruce Wayne, Batman puts his brilliant fighting and deductive skills to the test every night, inspiring dozens of other valiant men and women to do the same.

Nightwing

Dick Grayson started as Batman's sidekick, Robin, later graduating to life as a hero in his own right called Nightwing. Nightwing is one of Batgirl's oldest friends and a modern day swashbuckler, often defeating villains with a smile on his face.

Commissioner Gordon

James W. Gordon is Gotham City's top cop and Barbara Gordon's father. A devoted advocate of living a good and honest life, Gordon helped rid the Gotham City Police Department of untrustworthy police officers.

The Joker

The Joker is Batman's archenemy, but the so-called Clown Prince of Crime has had some run-ins with Batgirl as well. After he paralyzed the heroine for a short time, the Joker haunted her nightmares for years.

James Gordon Jr.

Barbara's little brother isn't quite cut from the same cloth as the rest of the moral, upstanding Gordon family. As an adult, James became one of Batgirl's most dangerous enemies.

Batwing

Luke Fox is a natural fighter chosen by Batman to wear the hi-tech costume of the hero Batwing. While he has put a hold on super heroics at the moment, Luke has nevertheless entered Barbara's life as her current boyfriend.

Black Canary

A fellow crime fighter and co-founder of the Super Hero team Birds of Prey, Black Canary uses her sonic scream and martial arts skills to team up with Batgirl and fight crime.

Chronology

Barbara Gordon is born to police officer James Gordon and his wife, Barbara Kean Gordon.

The Gordon family moves from Chicago to Gotham City.

While in college, Barbara tours the Gotham City Police Department, donning a police mock-up Batsuit to fight and defeat an escaping criminal, Harry X.

Barbara adopts the name Batgirl and a gray bodysuit, blue cape, and domino mask, beginning her career as a crime fighter.

The Joker shoots and paralyzes Barbara Gordon, yet she refuses to be defeated.

Barbara undergoes surgery to receive an experimental spinal implant.

As a teenager, Barbara excels
at everything from ballet to
martial arts.

When Batman debuts,
Barbara begins to idolize the
vigilante hero.

Batgirl is accepted into the
Dark Knight's ranks and
learns the secret identity of
Batman and Robin.

After messing up on the job,
Barbara retires from life as
Batgirl to concentrate on her
college studies.

Healed and able to walk
again, Barbara gets herself
back into fighting shape.

Barbara dons a new version
of her Batgirl costume,
a Batsuit equipped with
lightweight protective
armor.

Batgirl meets Black Canary while on a mission at the Penguin's Iceberg Casino.

Batgirl and Black Canary form a team of heroines called the Birds of Prey.

After her hero gear is destroyed in a fire, Batgirl decides to fight crime in her own unique way, creating a new costume in the process.

Batgirl battles an artificial intelligence program that she had designed years ago while paralyzed.

Barbara Gordon starts a new company called Gordon Clean Energy while continuing to look toward her equally bright future as Batgirl.

Batgirl battles a new breed of villains, including Knightfall and her associates Gretel and the Mirror.

Barbara leaves Gotham City proper in favor of one of its boroughs, Burnside.

Barbara Gordon begins to date Luke Fox, the hero known as Batwing.

A villain named the Fugue pits nearly all of Batgirl's biggest villains against her. Batgirl manages to triumph over the foe with a little help from her friends.

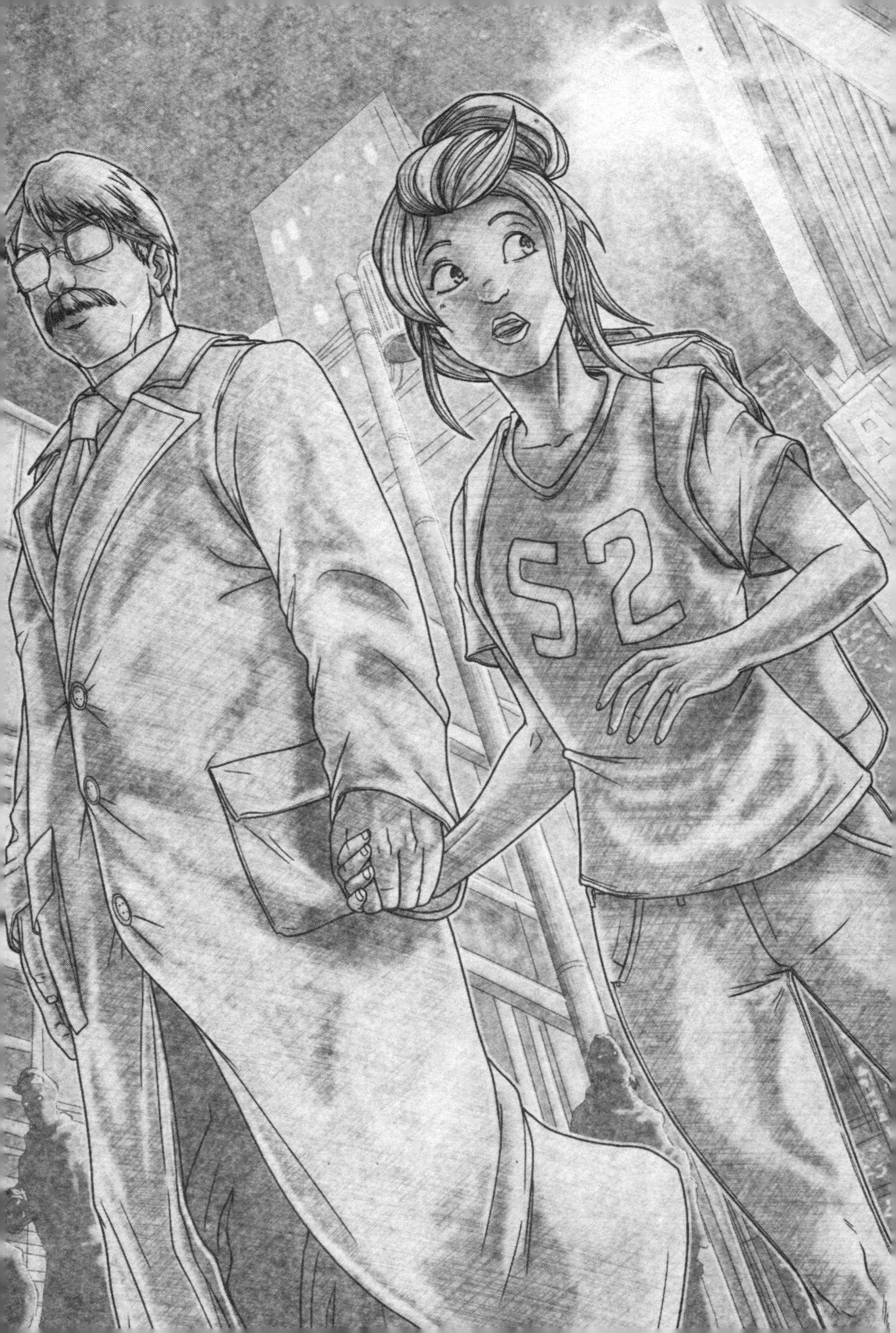
52

CHAPTER ONE

BEFORE BATGIRL

When Lieutenant James Gordon moved his family from Chicago to Gotham City, he had no idea how drastically he was about to change the life of his daughter Barbara. James Gordon was an honest cop with a desire to make something of himself. He believed that opportunities had dried up for him in his hometown of Chicago. Gotham City seemed like the kind of town where he could make a real impact. But the one thing that Gordon had failed to realize was just how corrupt

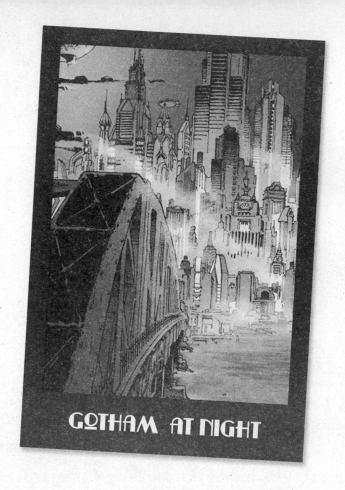

GOTHAM AT NIGHT

this new city truly was.

Over half the cops in the Gotham City Police Department were making secret deals with various criminal organizations. Even Police Commissioner Gillian Loeb worked hand in hand with dangerous criminals—but that didn't stop James Gordon from

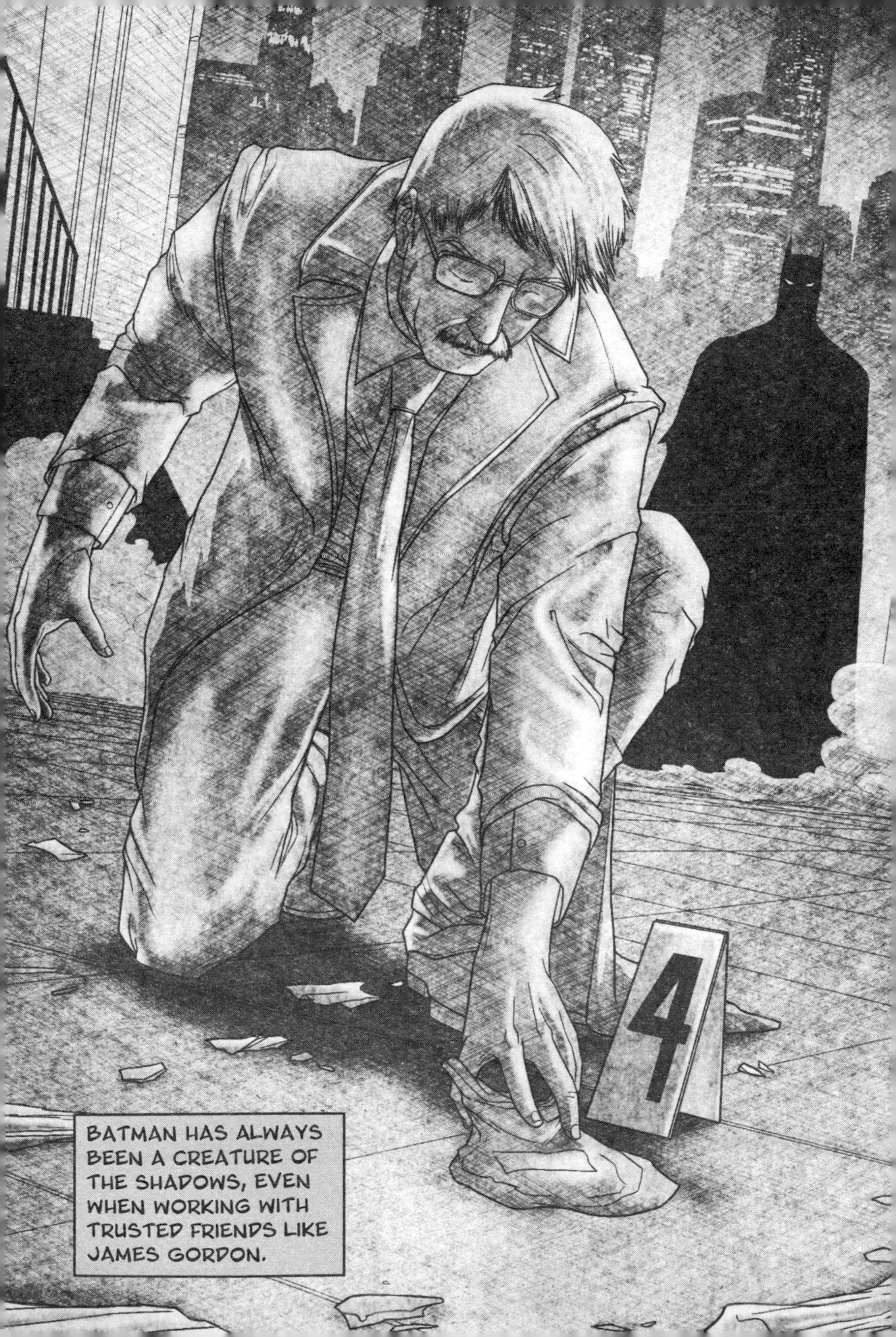
BATMAN HAS ALWAYS BEEN A CREATURE OF THE SHADOWS, EVEN WHEN WORKING WITH TRUSTED FRIENDS LIKE JAMES GORDON.
4

fighting for a better city. He saw to the capture of the Black Mask Gang, a group of masked criminals working for a wealthy businessman. He arrested many corrupt police officers, including the GCPD internal affairs officer Zachary Henshaw. Though he was reluctant about it at first, James Gordon even began working with a vigilante who had appeared in Gotham City: a mysterious masked man in a cape whom the press called Batman.

Gordon rose through the ranks of the Gotham City Police Department and was declared a hero by the public. But his biggest fan lived at home with him. His daughter Barbara was an extremely intelligent teenager who had idolized her father for as long as she could remember—and she could remember quite a lot. She possessed an eidetic memory—also known as a photographic memory—and could recall events from her past with incredible accuracy and detail. Barbara had long recognized her father for the hero he was, and her dad doted on her in return.

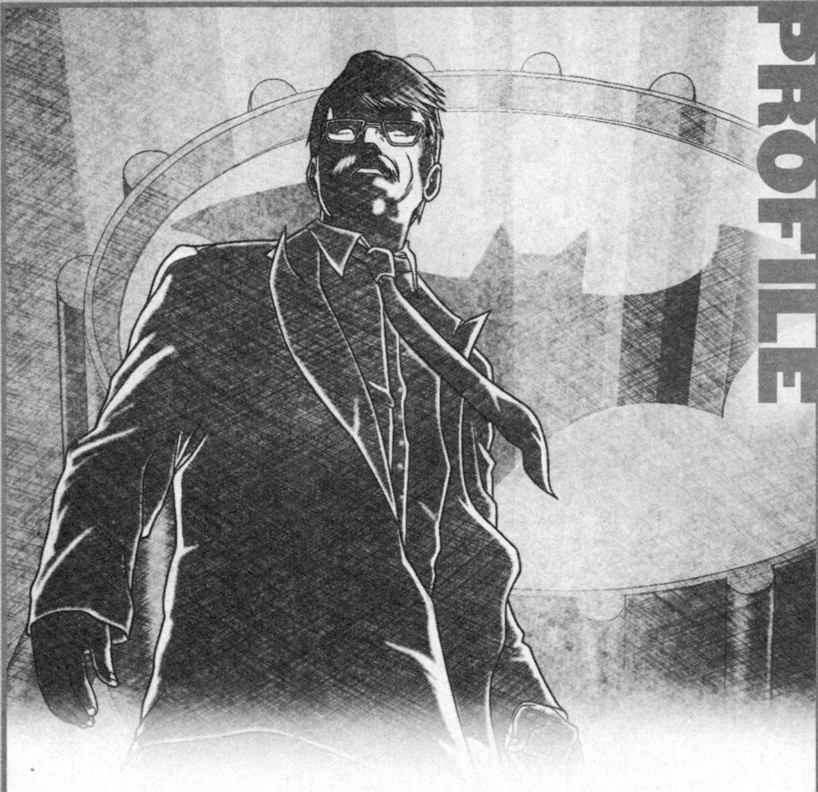
PROFILE

Commissioner James Gordon

With a strong sense of ethics and a tough stance against crime, Commissioner James Gordon's only weakness seems to be his daughter Barbara. Gordon is a true hero who worked his way up the Gotham City Police Department from lieutenant to commissioner. He has formed a strong bond with Barbara, perhaps seeing his own determination reflected in her eyes. Gordon has never learned about his own daughter's double identity. He is simply content to see her happy and healthy, willing to let her lead her own life and make her own choices.

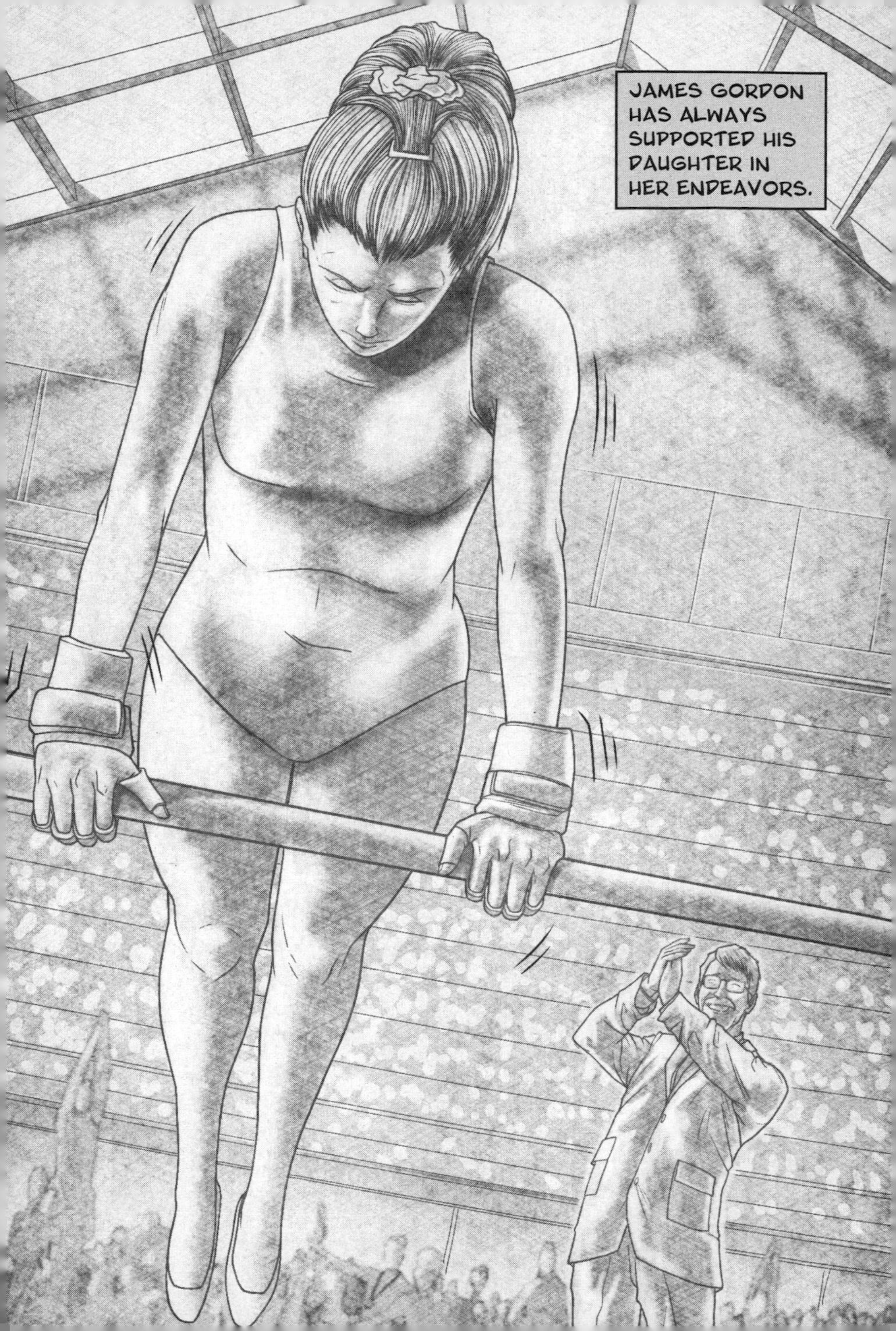
JAMES GORDON HAS ALWAYS SUPPORTED HIS DAUGHTER IN HER ENDEAVORS.

She developed a desire to impress him and prove herself capable of overcoming any challenge. She studied various martial arts, taking a particular interest in judo, as well as ballet, gymnastics, and criminology. She tacked up her father's newspaper clippings on her bedroom wall, hoping to one day be just like him—though there was someone else who fascinated her, too: the Caped Crusader known as Batman.

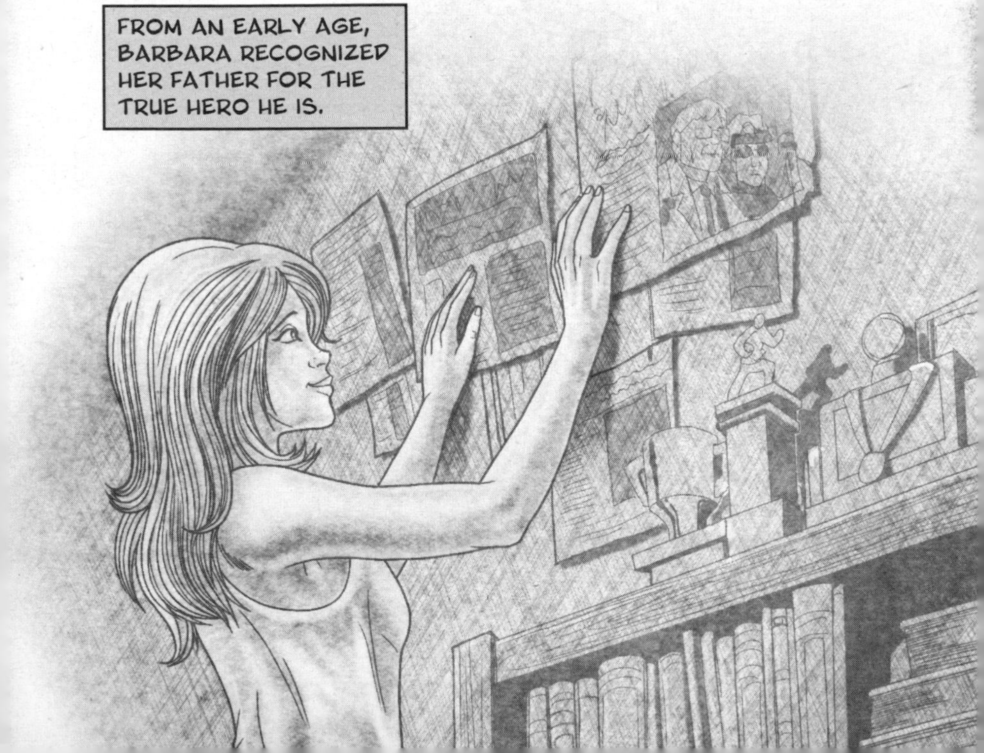
FROM AN EARLY AGE, BARBARA RECOGNIZED HER FATHER FOR THE TRUE HERO HE IS.

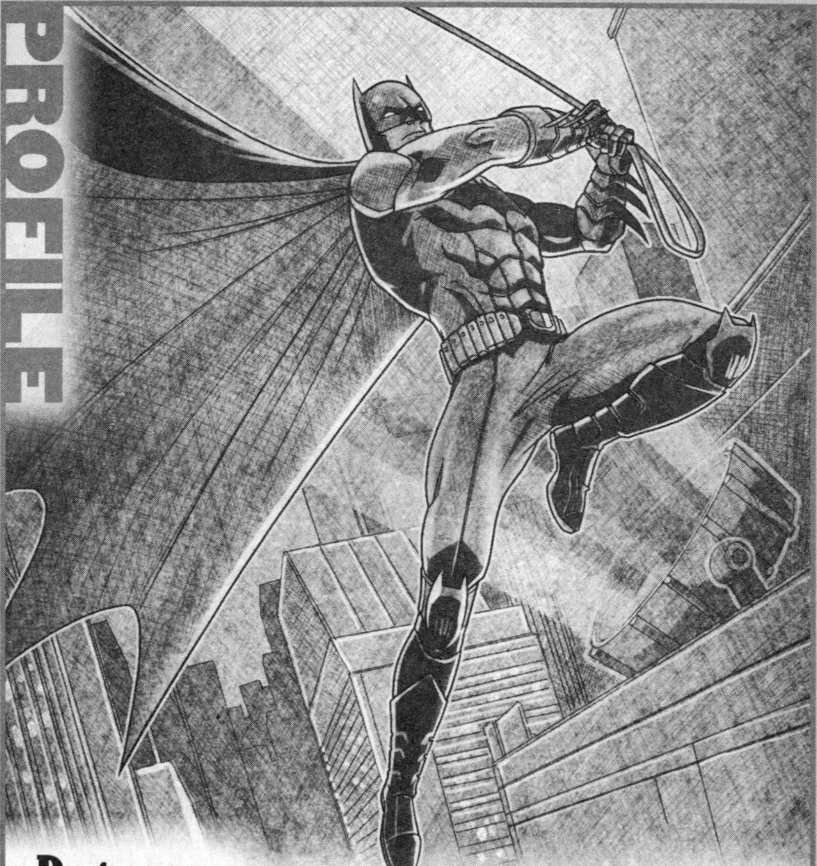
PROFILE

Batman

When Bruce Wayne was just a boy, his parents were killed. On the night his parents were buried, Bruce swore that no other innocent person would suffer the way he had been forced to. He traveled the world, learning from police detectives, accomplished actors, escape artists, inventors, and martial artists. He then returned to Gotham City as Batman, a Super Hero relying on nothing but his wits, technology, and skills to combat some of the most dangerous criminals the world has ever seen.

Barbara didn't know much about this mysterious crime fighter, aside from what she read in the papers. Batman first emerged when a group of criminals called the Red Hood Gang terrorized Gotham City, and he eventually took down their entire organization. Batman was as heroic as James Gordon, but he was also something more. He worked outside the law. That meant he wasn't subject to the rules and politics she often heard her father complaining about. Barbara found that even more exciting than the life her father led. Batman seemed one with Gotham City, and Barbara often found herself fantasizing about leaping over rooftops and righting her city's wrongs.

Not all of James Gordon's family took to Gotham City as well as Barbara did. The town seemed to only further push Barbara's little brother James over the edge. James Gordon Jr. lacked empathy for others. He hated his parents for praising Barbara's achievements and plotted to break up his family—and he managed to do just that when he drove his own mother away

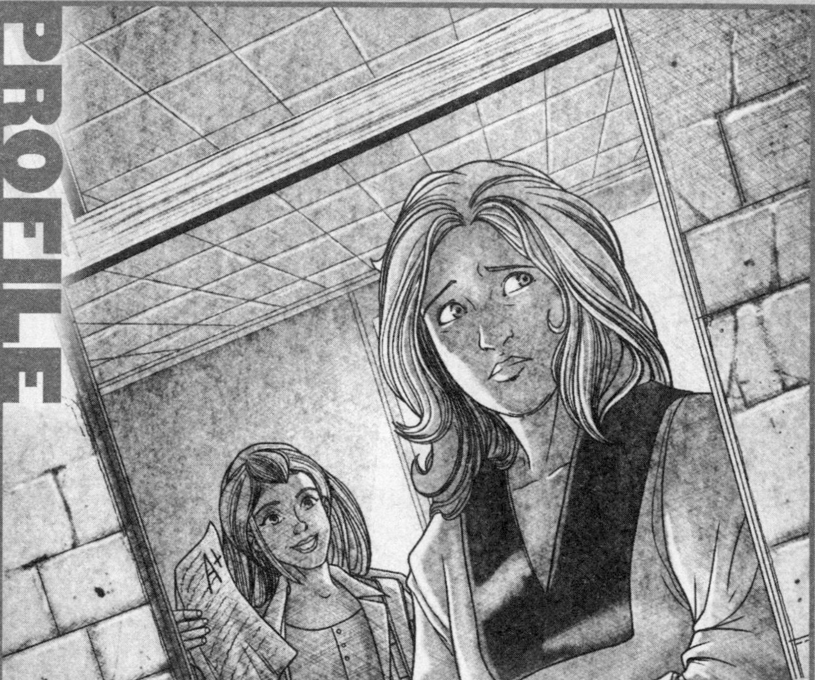
PROFILE

Barbara Kean Gordon

From the start, Barbara Kean Gordon was hesitant to relocate to Gotham City, but she tried to make the best of it for the sake of her two children. When her son began to show signs of a mental problem, the stress proved too much for Barbara, and she abandoned her family. She recently returned to her daughter's life for a brief time, taking the first step in healing old wounds.

with his disturbing antics. Scared of the evil she saw in her own son's eyes, the elder Barbara left her family behind, not to return for years.

Though it was a strain on their family when Barbara Kean left, James Gordon and his daughter grew even closer as a result. Barbara tried to involve James Jr. more in their activities. She truly wanted the best for her brother despite his oddly cold demeanor. The two siblings found a common love of horror movies, although they seemed to enjoy them for different reasons.

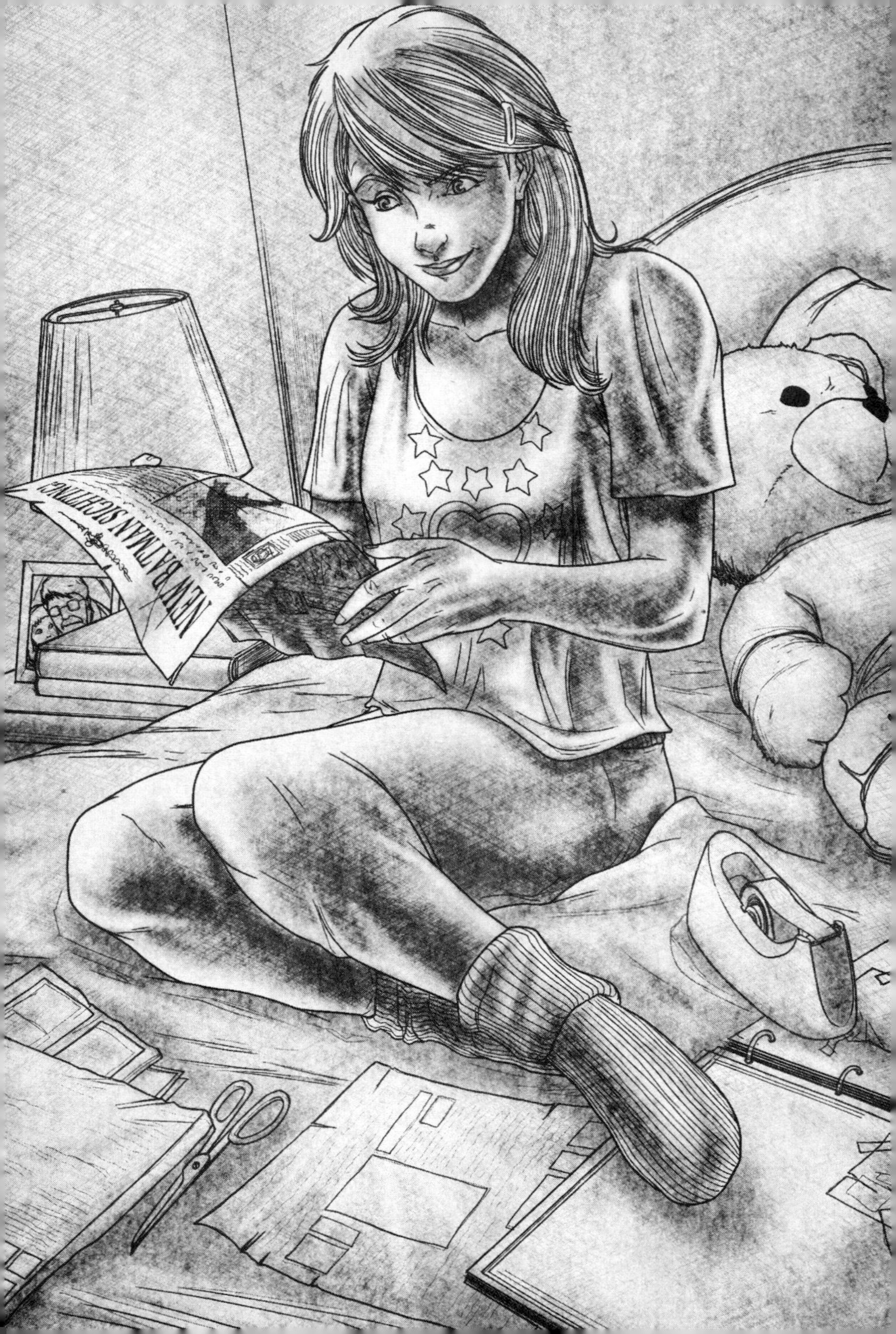
NEW BATMAN SIGHTING?

Years of walking in her father's footsteps had set Barbara off on the right path. Studying the actions of Batman continued to spark her interest in helping the people of her city. She had mastered dozens of valuable skills by the time she was in college, but Barbara still lacked direction. Soon, a routine visit to her father's police precinct would chart the course for the rest of her life.

BARBARA COLLECTED
NEWSPAPER CLIPPINGS
ABOUT BATMAN'S
ADVENTURES AROUND
GOTHAM CITY.

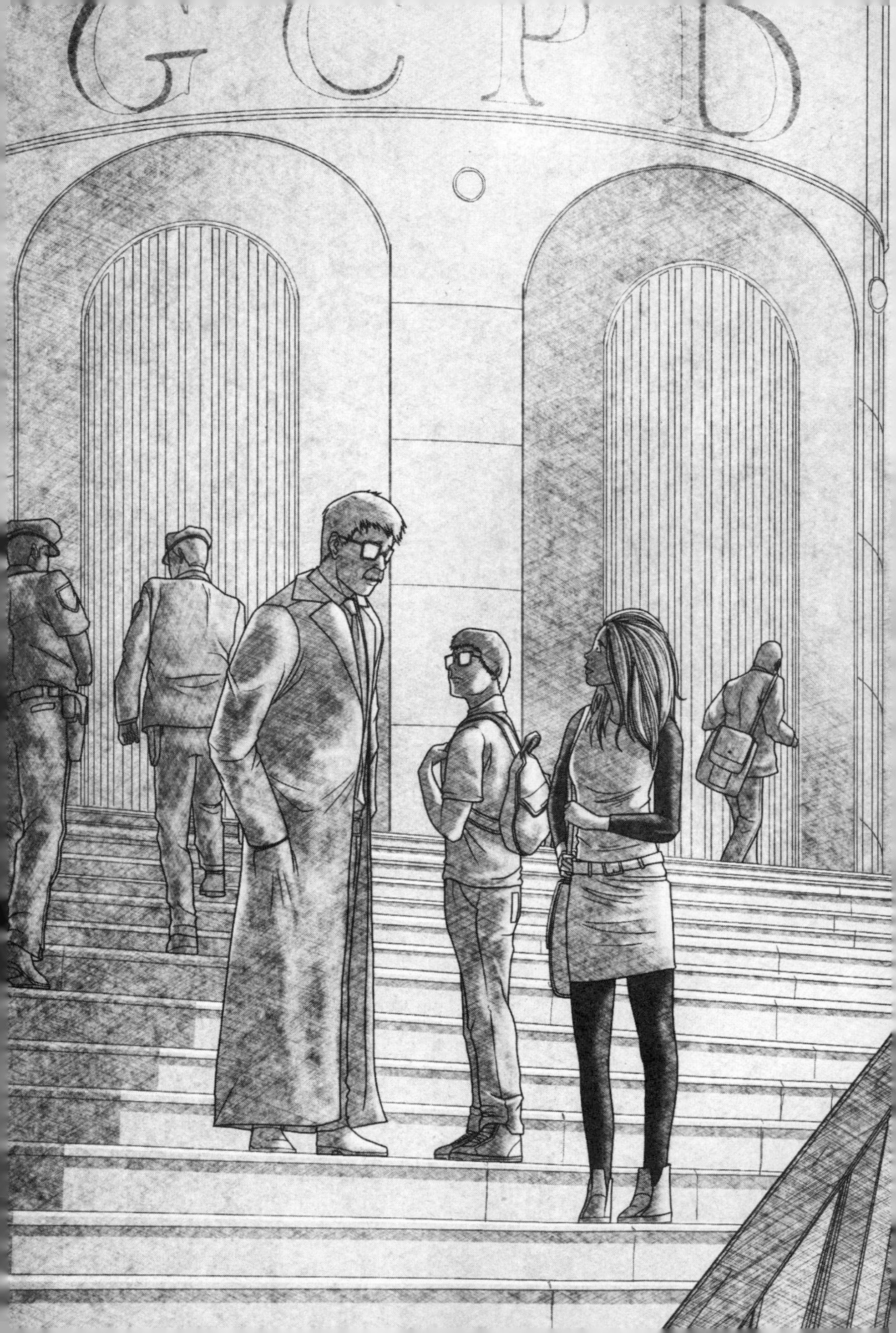
GCPD

CHAPTER TWO

THE FIRST BATTLE

While in college, Barbara Gordon knew she had a built-in advantage when she signed up for Intro to Criminology. Her father had become the commissioner of the Gotham City Police Department. She knew the best way to land an "A" was to visit her dad at work and learn some of the ins and outs of being a cop in Gotham City. While her father agreed to give her a tour alongside her little brother, James Jr., what Commissioner Gordon didn't realize was that Barbara had an ulterior motive

GCPD VISITOR

Barbara Gordon
Visitor's Pass

BARBARA Gordon

for visiting the GCPD. What she really wanted to learn was the scoop on Gotham's secretive vigilante, Batman.

At the police precinct, Officer Dwight Morgan gave the Gordon siblings a tour. Along the way, Barbara began interviewing every member of the GCPD she came across. It took a while, but finally

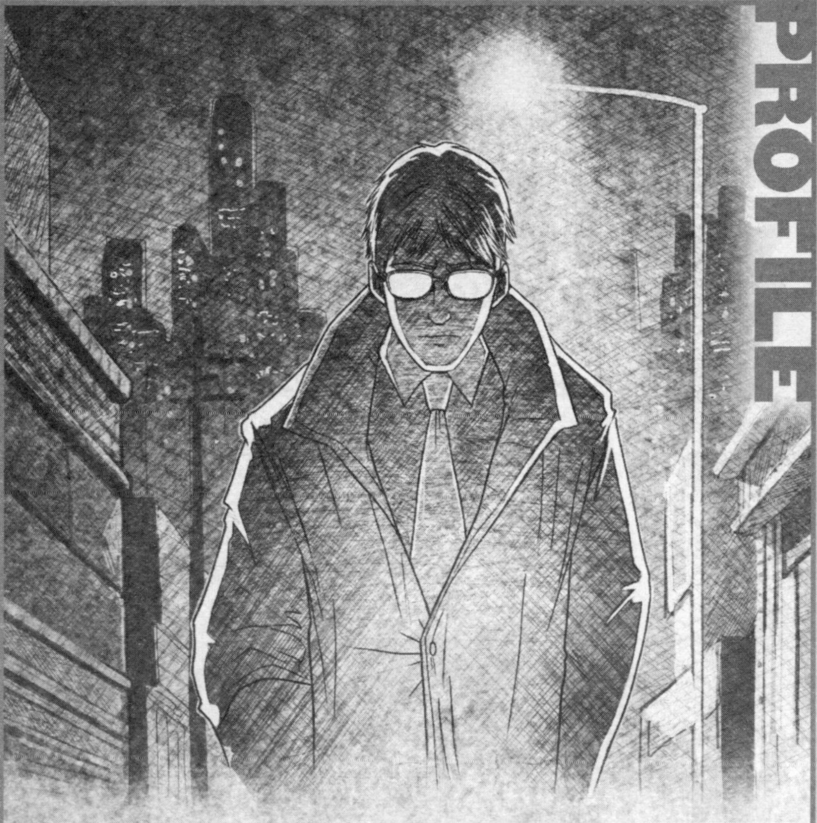
PROFILE

James Gordon Jr.

Ever since he was a little boy, James Gordon Jr. observed the world around him with a critical eye, but he kept his complex thoughts to himself. James was there the day Barbara Gordon first donned a Batsuit inside the Gotham City Police Department, so he's in on secret that Barbara is Batgirl. However, while he has grown to despise his sister, James prefers to keep his knowledge to himself. He has been plotting Barbara's downfall since his youth and enjoys the idea of personally making her life miserable.

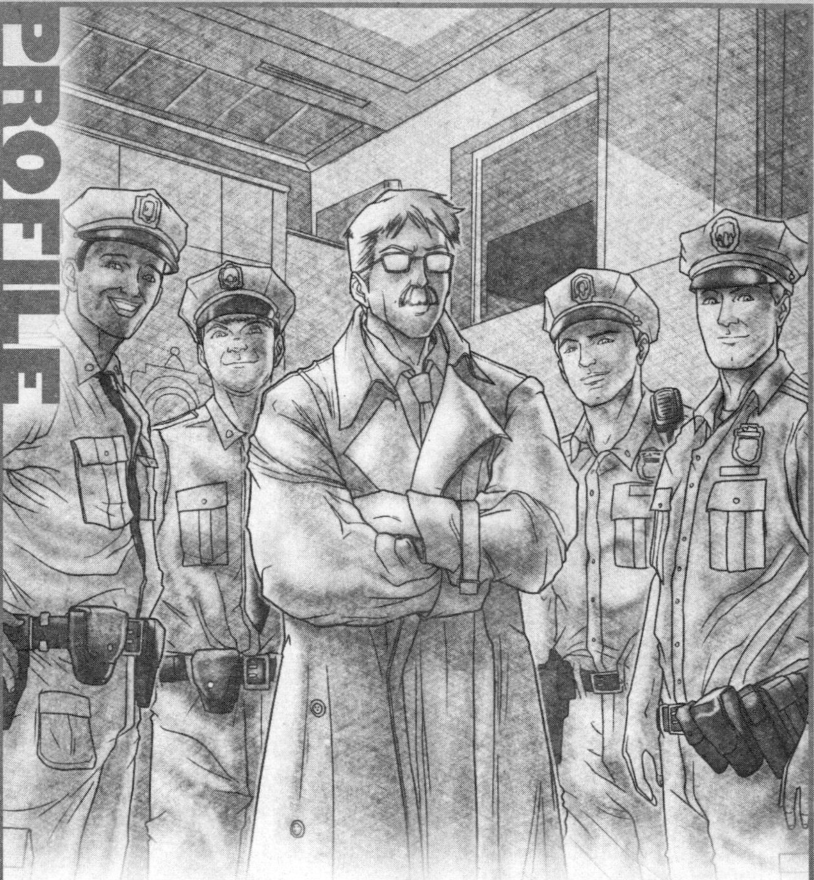
PROFILE

Gotham City Police Department

The Gotham City Police Department, or GCPD for short, has a long-standing history of corruption at the highest level. While its officers swear an oath to serve the people of the city, most can't resist the bribes offered to them by Gotham's many criminals. Commissioner James Gordon is an exception to that rule. Ever since his rise to the top of the GCPD, he has made significant progress in cleaning up the department.

Barbara found what she was looking for: the office of the Batman Task Force.

At that time, most people in Gotham City didn't believe that Batman truly existed. They assumed he was an urban myth told to frighten criminals or kids who refused to go to bed at night. Nonetheless, the GCPD had been taking the threat of a rogue vigilante quite seriously. As Barbara discovered, the police had even formed a task force to shut down Batman once and for all.

As Barbara peered into the task force's office, she saw a prototype Batsuit that the officers had put together based on eyewitness testimonies of Batman sightings. The suit was black and gray, complete with a black cowl, matching cape, and a bulletproof vest. Barbara listened as the officers talked about Batman utilizing high-tech gadgets like goggles that allowed him to see in the dark and an oxygen rebreather that he could use to filter out gas or swim underwater for long periods of time. It was at that point that Barbara

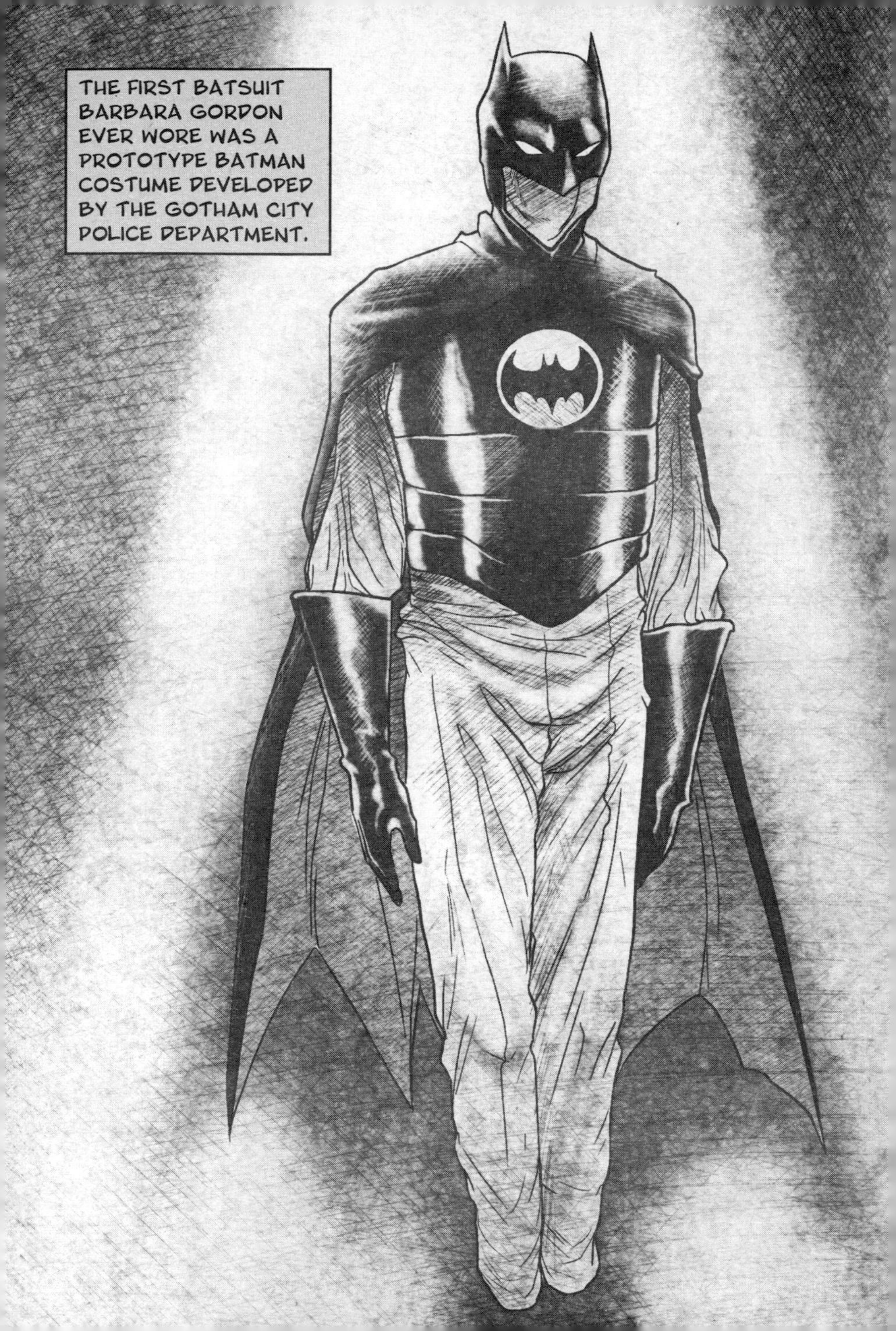
THE FIRST BATSUIT BARBARA GORDON EVER WORE WAS A PROTOTYPE BATMAN COSTUME DEVELOPED BY THE GOTHAM CITY POLICE DEPARTMENT.

realized Batman wasn't a mythical creature with superhuman powers and abilities—he was just like her. He relied on his wits above all else.

Barbara's education on Super Heroes quickly came to a crashing halt. Before she could eavesdrop any longer, she was interrupted by the super-villain called Harry X. Seemingly in secure police custody, Harry X was being escorted through the precinct past Barbara and her brother. The murderer was awaiting a possible transfer back to his home country of Canada. Unfortunately for the GCPD, Harry X had other plans.

Suddenly, there was an explosion in the police precinct. The room filled with smoke and fire as Harry X's devoted followers burst in. They unchained him as Barbara and James Jr. ran for cover. But Harry X wasn't about to let Barbara get away. He needed a hostage in order to escape the heavily guarded building. Barbara and James fled but eventually became separated when tear gas flooded the floor.

THE NOTORIOUS HARRY X.

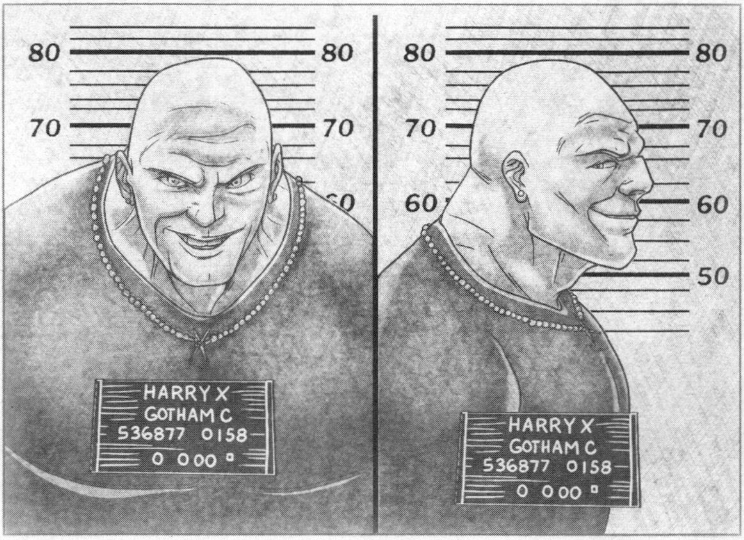
80
70
HARRY X
GOTHAM C
536877 0158
0 000
HARRY X
GOTHAM C
536877 0158
0 000

It was then that Barbara made a decision that would affect the rest of her life.

Barbara made her way inside the office of the Batman Task Force. She quickly donned the GCPD's makeshift Batman costume, arming herself with two police batons. Then she confronted Harry X head-on. Using her lifetime of martial arts training, Barbara managed to defeat the much larger Harry X, knocking the super-villain out with a final blow to the head.

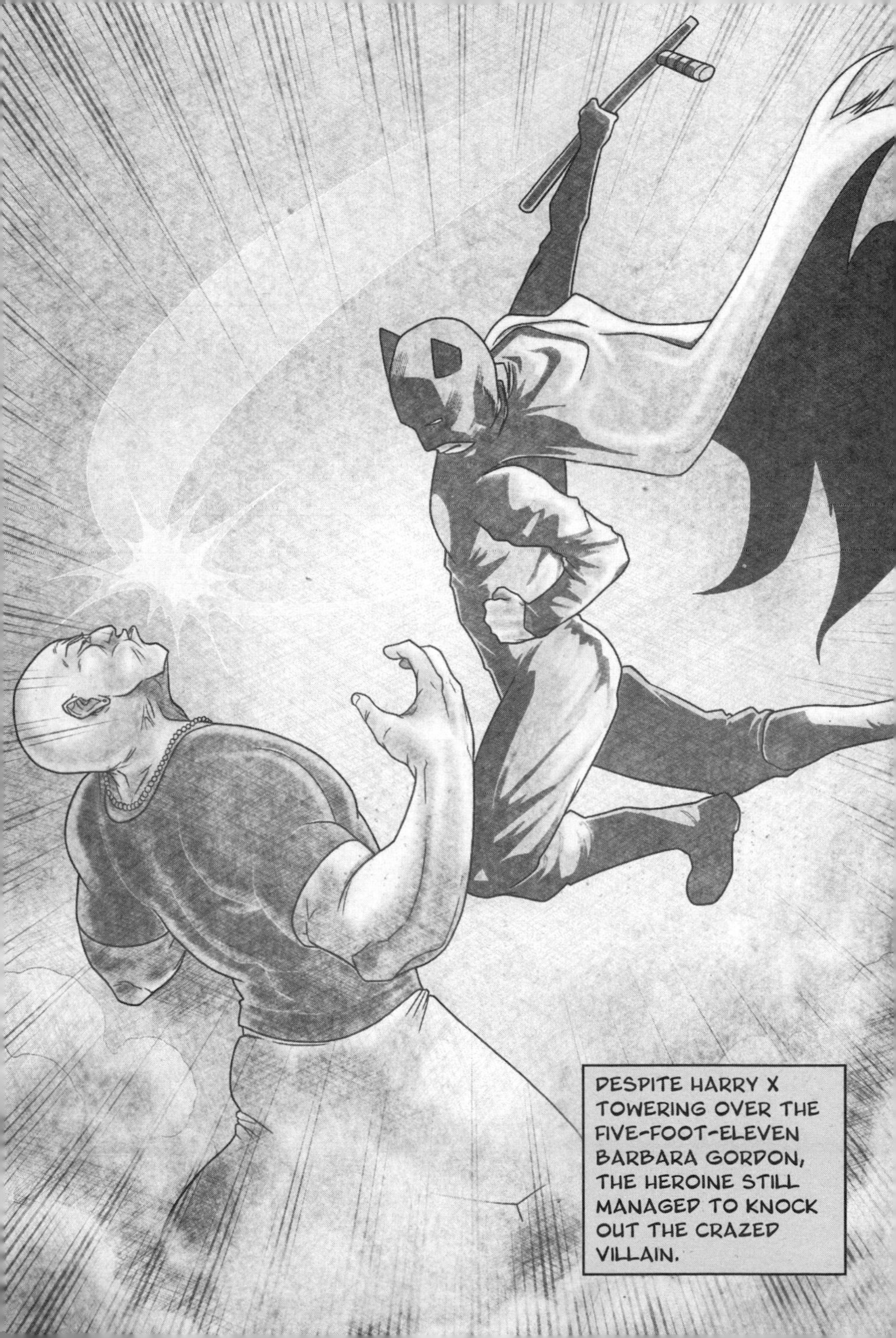
DESPITE HARRY X TOWERING OVER THE FIVE-FOOT-ELEVEN BARBARA GORDON, THE HEROINE STILL MANAGED TO KNOCK OUT THE CRAZED VILLAIN.

BARBARA GORDON'S ROUGH SKETCH OF BATMAN, DRAWN SHORTLY AFTER THEIR FIRST MEETING.

As she rested against a wall, another figure appeared in the dense smoke. It was the real Batman. He looked at Barbara and at the bulky man unconscious on the ground. Then he said something that he almost never said: "Nice work."

Batman faded back into the shadows, disappearing as mysteriously as he had arrived. The world looked like a different place to Barbara that night. Everything finally made sense. The next day, she began designing a costume of her own—and Batgirl was born.

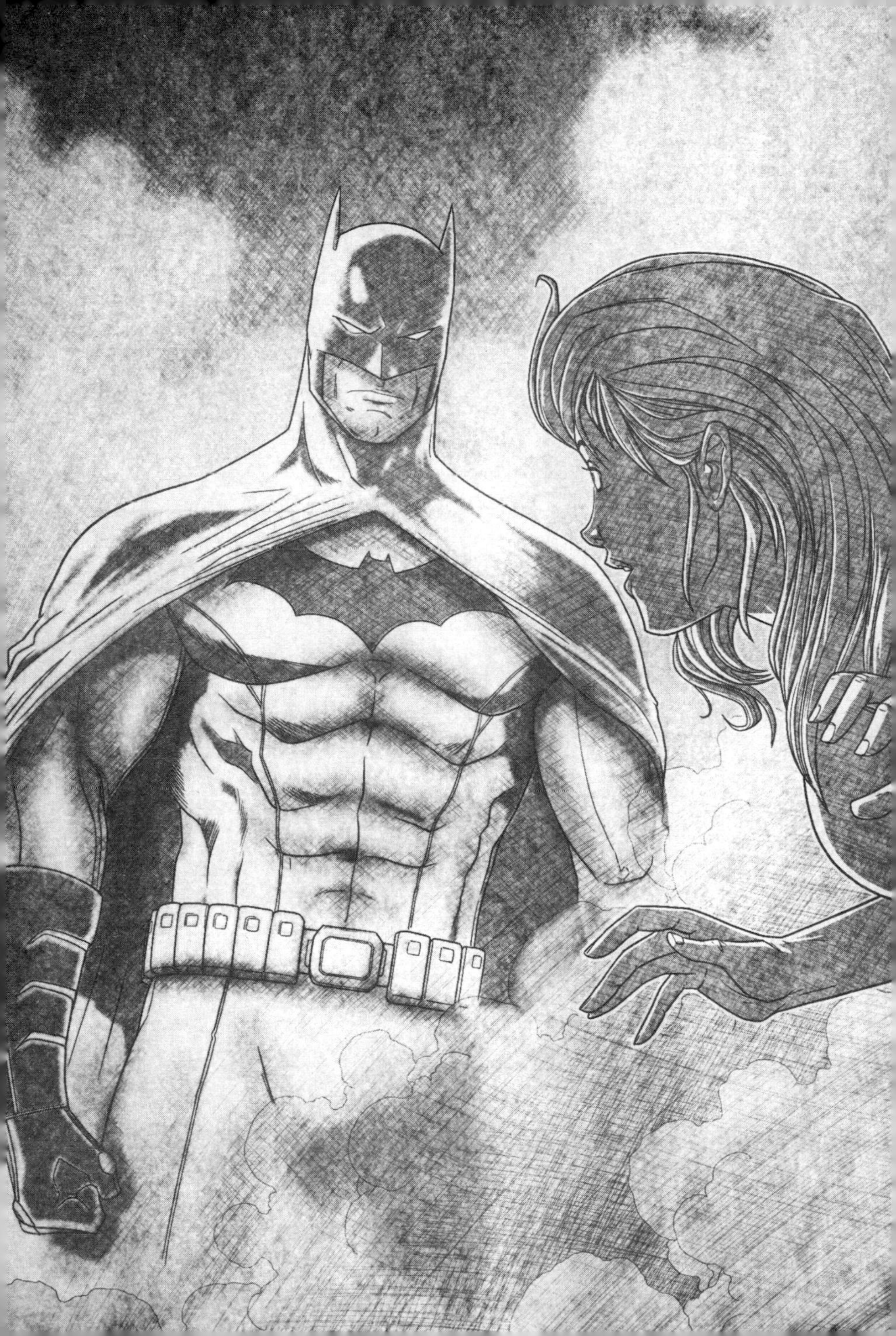

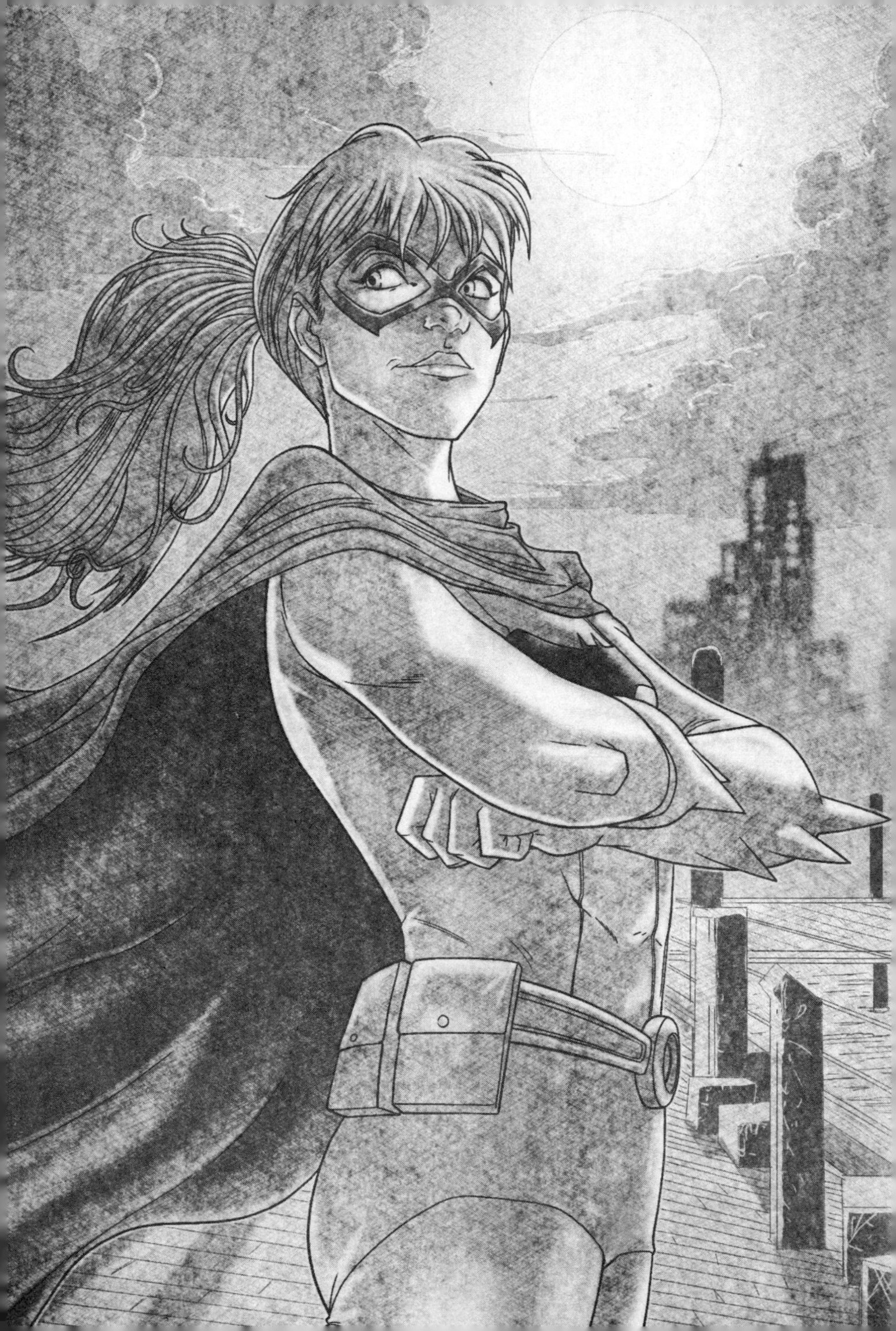

CHAPTER THREE

THE EARLY YEARS

Defeating Harry X at the Gotham City Police Department had shown Barbara just how effective she could be, no matter how the odds were stacked against her. She'd seen the good she could do in the world and was hooked. Barbara realized that she'd need to shield her identity from the public to protect not only herself, but also the life and career of her father. She designed her own Batsuit to wear as a disguise: a gray bodysuit adorned with the famous black bat-symbol, a blue cape, yellow gloves and matching Utility Belt, and a gray domino mask.

Without Batman's approval, a new vigilante, Batgirl, was born. And like her mentor, she immediately threw herself into the thick of things.

BATGIRL'S ORIGINAL DOMINO MASK.

She fought armed criminals, saved infants from burning buildings, and battled deadly assassins. She trained herself on the job, learning how to scale buildings and swing across the rooftops on a thin line. Batgirl excelled at her new vocation. She was soon giving even Batman's young crime-fighting partner, Robin, a run for his money.

Batman was wary of taking on another young partner. Though he saw Batgirl's natural talent, he insisted she give up her attempt at imitating him. But Barbara took Batman's criticism as a challenge and began to work harder at her Super Hero career. Nearly a year after Batgirl first appeared on the scene, Batman finally accepted the inevitable and officially let her into his "family." Both he and Robin shared their secret identities with Barbara, and, for a while, things went exactly as she had hoped. She fought some of the most infamous criminals in Gotham City: from madmen like the Joker and Two-Face to hardened criminals like the Penguin and Riddler.

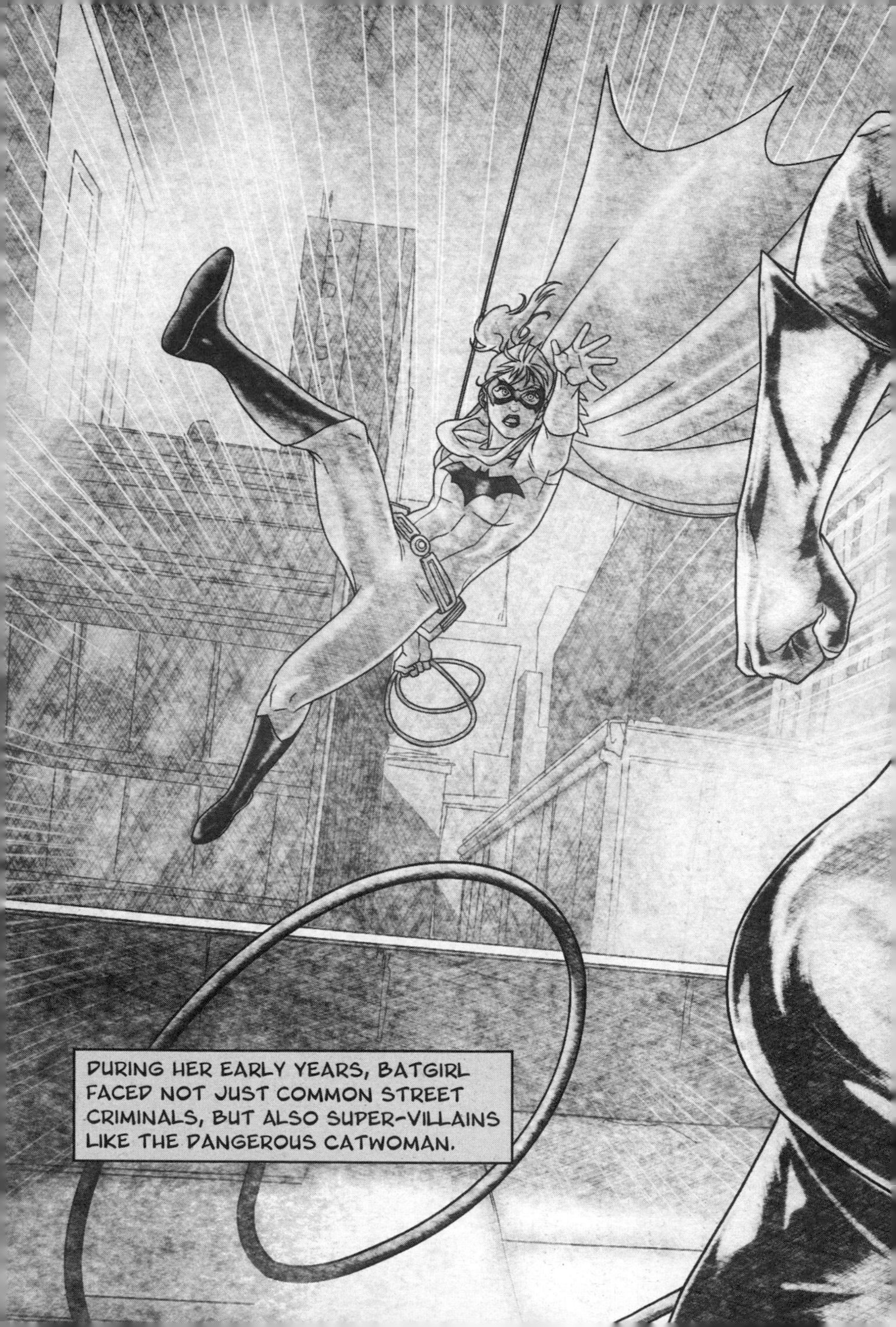
DURING HER EARLY YEARS, BATGIRL FACED NOT JUST COMMON STREET CRIMINALS, BUT ALSO SUPER-VILLAINS LIKE THE DANGEROUS CATWOMAN.

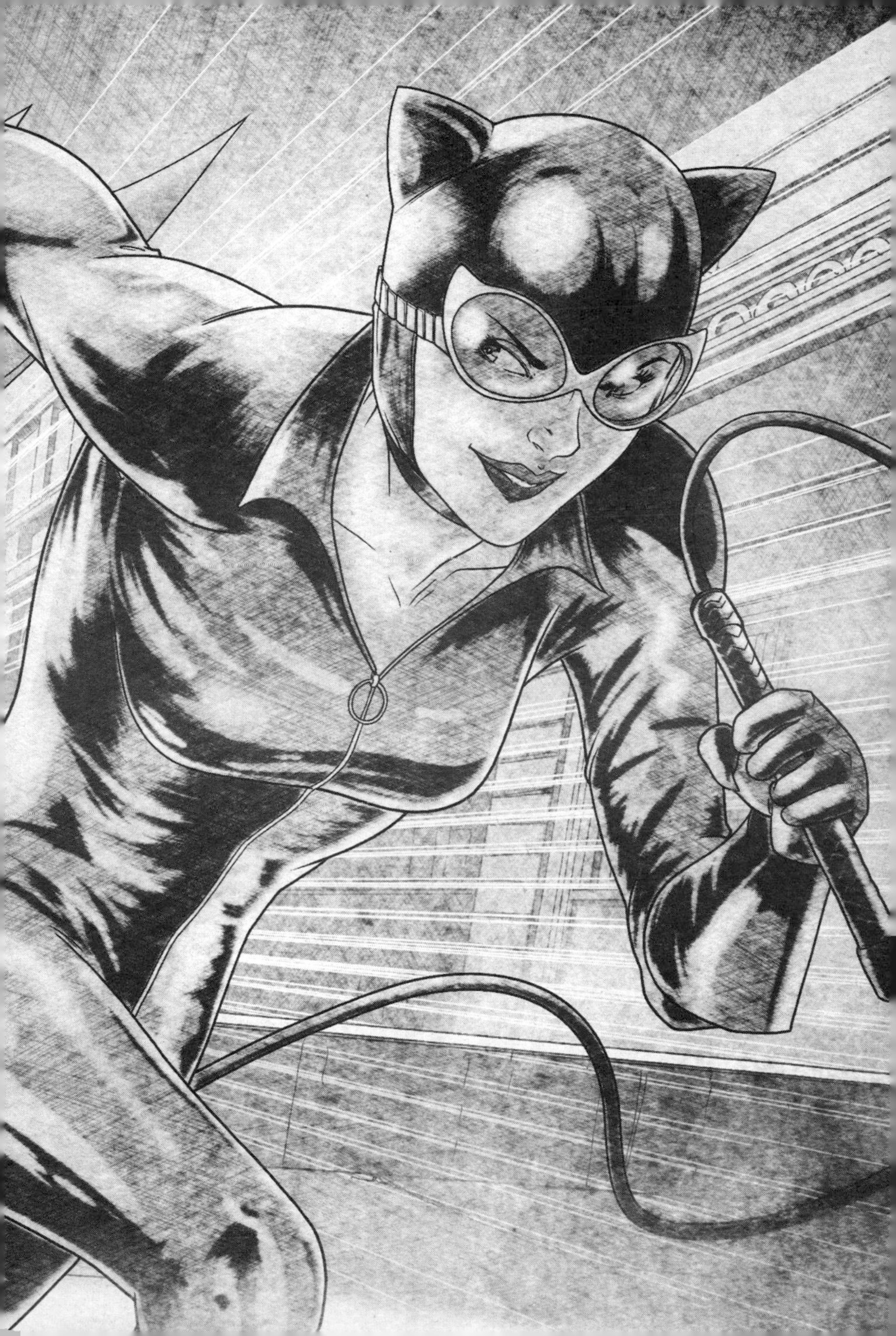

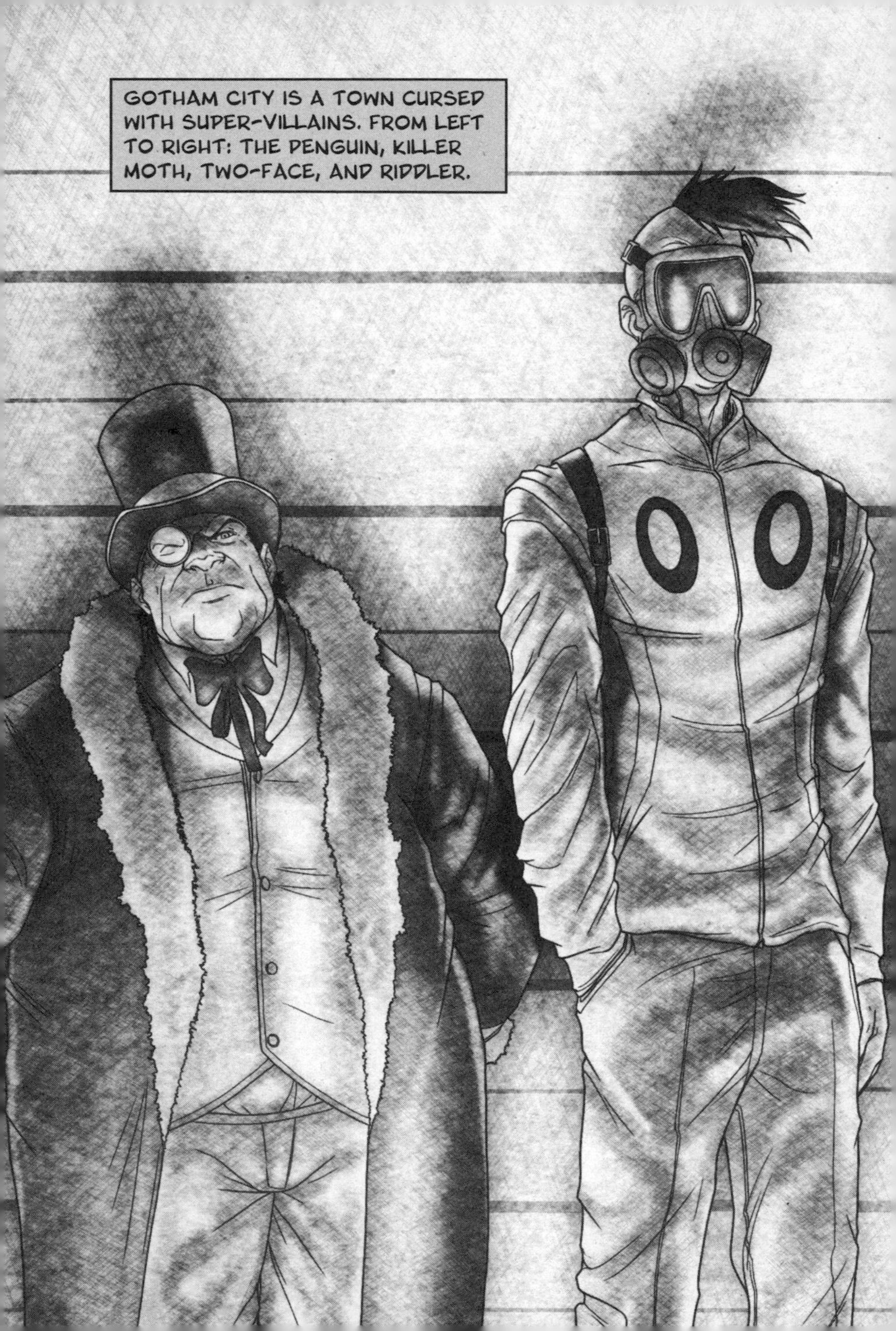
GOTHAM CITY IS A TOWN CURSED WITH SUPER-VILLAINS. FROM LEFT TO RIGHT: THE PENGUIN, KILLER MOTH, TWO-FACE, AND RIDDLER.

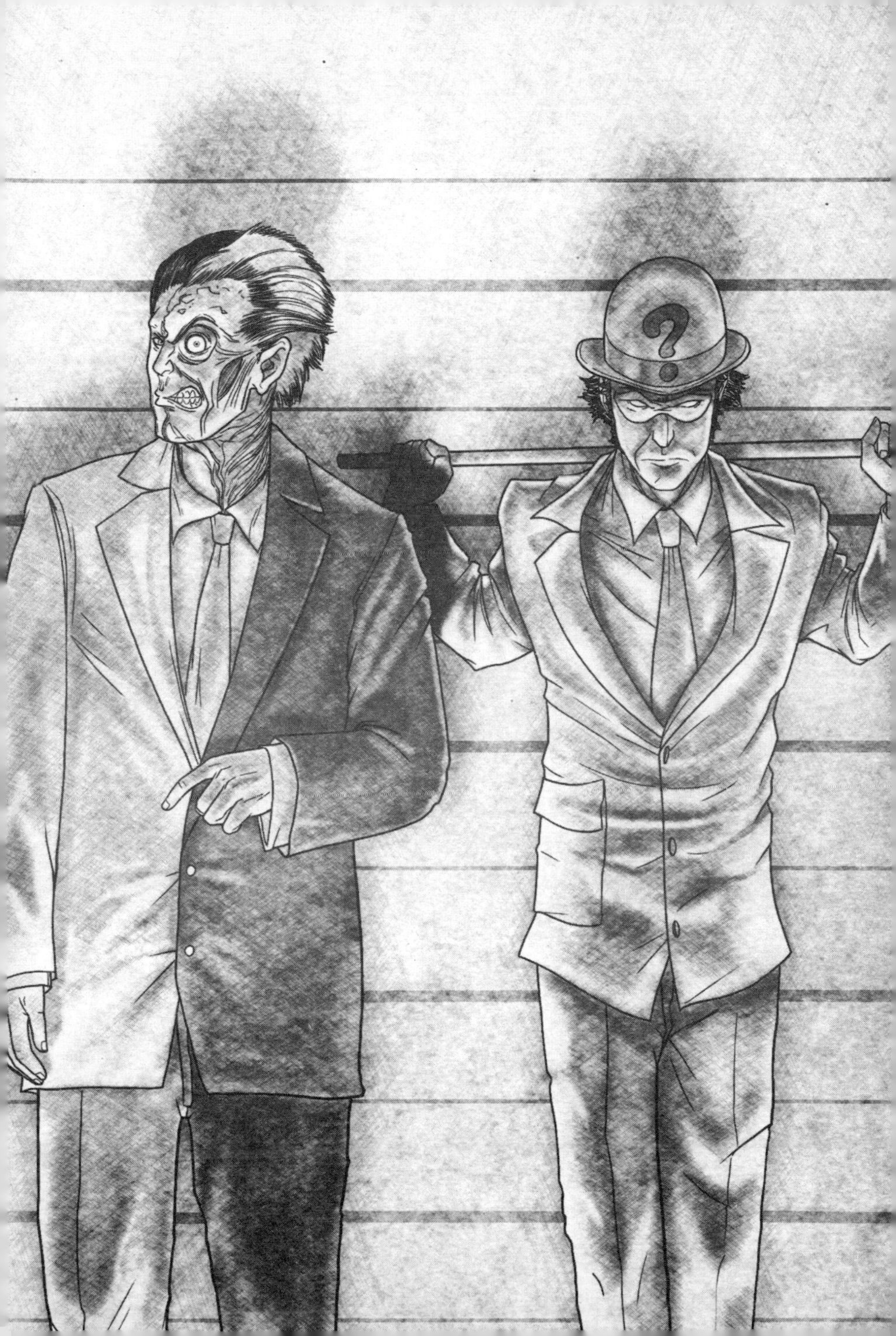

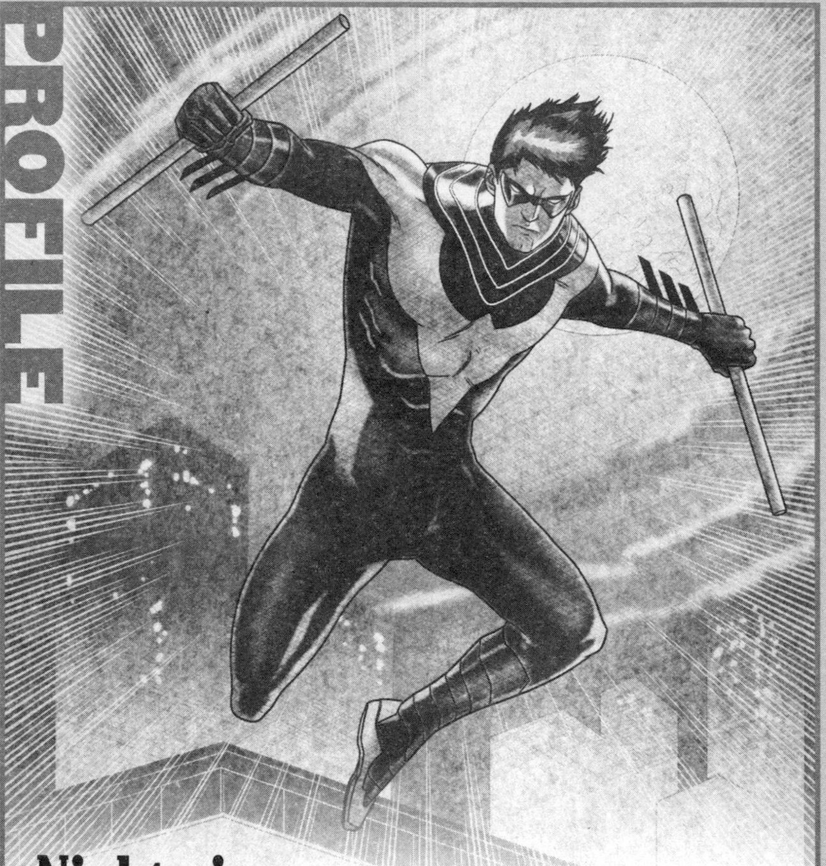
PROFILE

Nightwing

Dick Grayson went from being a circus performer to Batman's partner Robin in the blink of an eye. After Dick's parents were killed during their trapeze act, Bruce Wayne adopted the teenager as his ward. When Dick learned of Bruce's double life, the two became the Dynamic Duo of Batman and Robin. Dick Grayson later graduated to a life of solo crime fighting as Nightwing. Ever since they first met as Robin and Batgirl, Dick Grayson and Barbara Gordon have shared a close relationship.

Batgirl battled them all and continued to prove her worth as Batman's partner—until the one night she didn't.

The reason that Batgirl decided to hang up her cowl and cape remains a secret shared only by Batgirl,

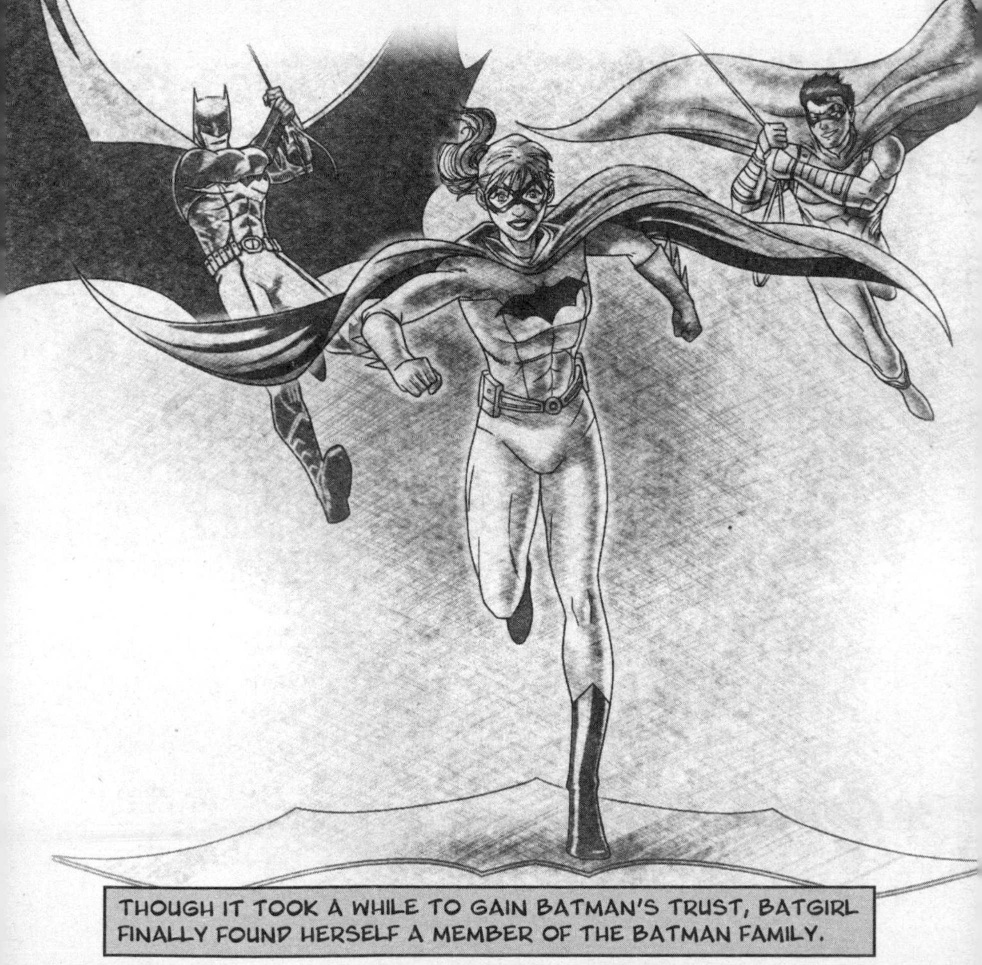
THOUGH IT TOOK A WHILE TO GAIN BATMAN'S TRUST, BATGIRL FINALLY FOUND HERSELF A MEMBER OF THE BATMAN FAMILY.

A BATARANG, ONE OF THE MANY TOOLS OF THE TRADE BATGIRL ADOPTED FROM HER MENTOR, BATMAN.

Batman, and Robin. All that is known about this mystery is that on one fateful night, Batgirl made a mistake while in the field that haunted her for many nights to come. Barbara Gordon decided to retire from a life of fighting crime and threw herself back into her college studies. She began dating and tried to forget about her life as Batgirl. But Gotham City was not done with her yet. Barbara Gordon would soon face her greatest challenge.

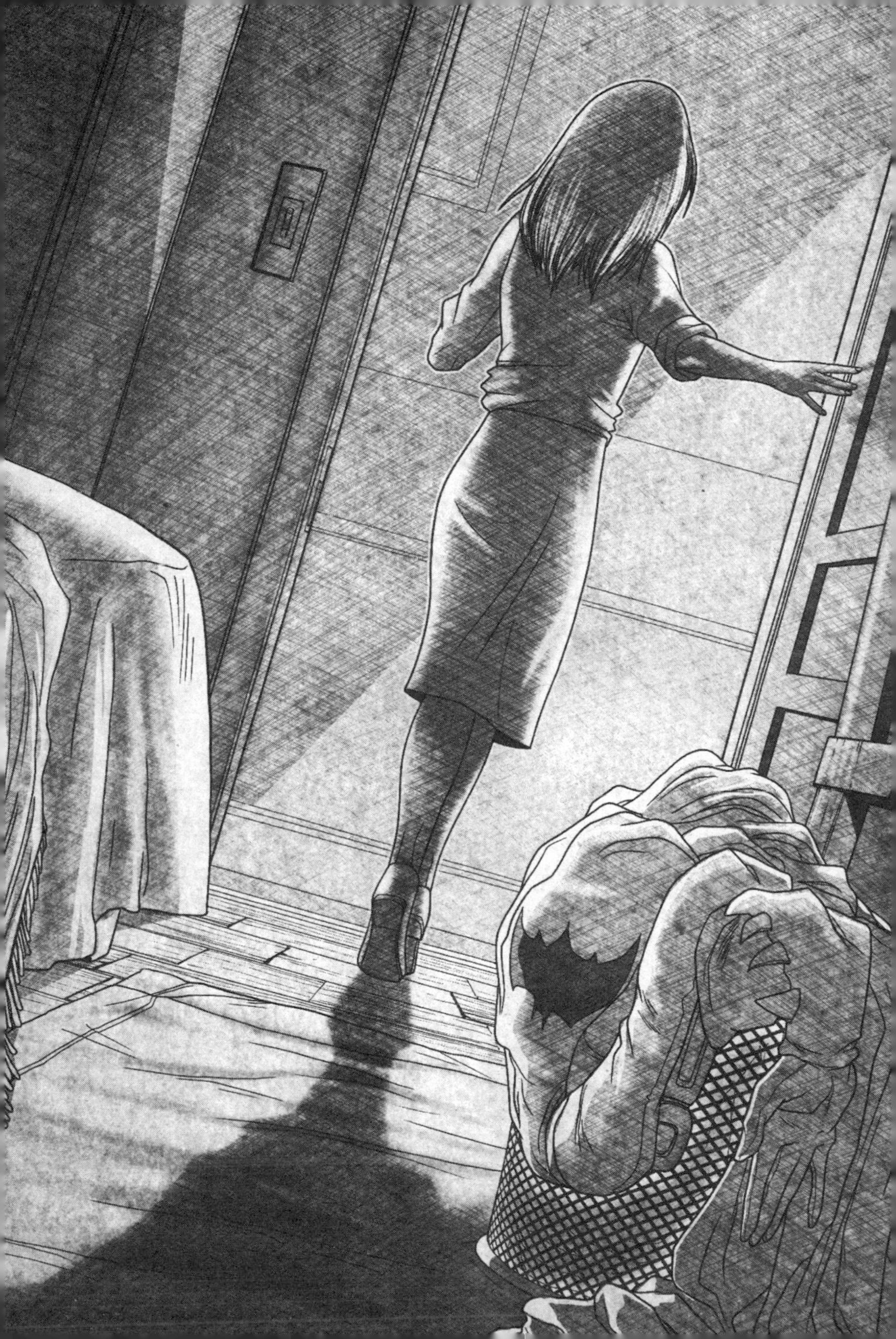

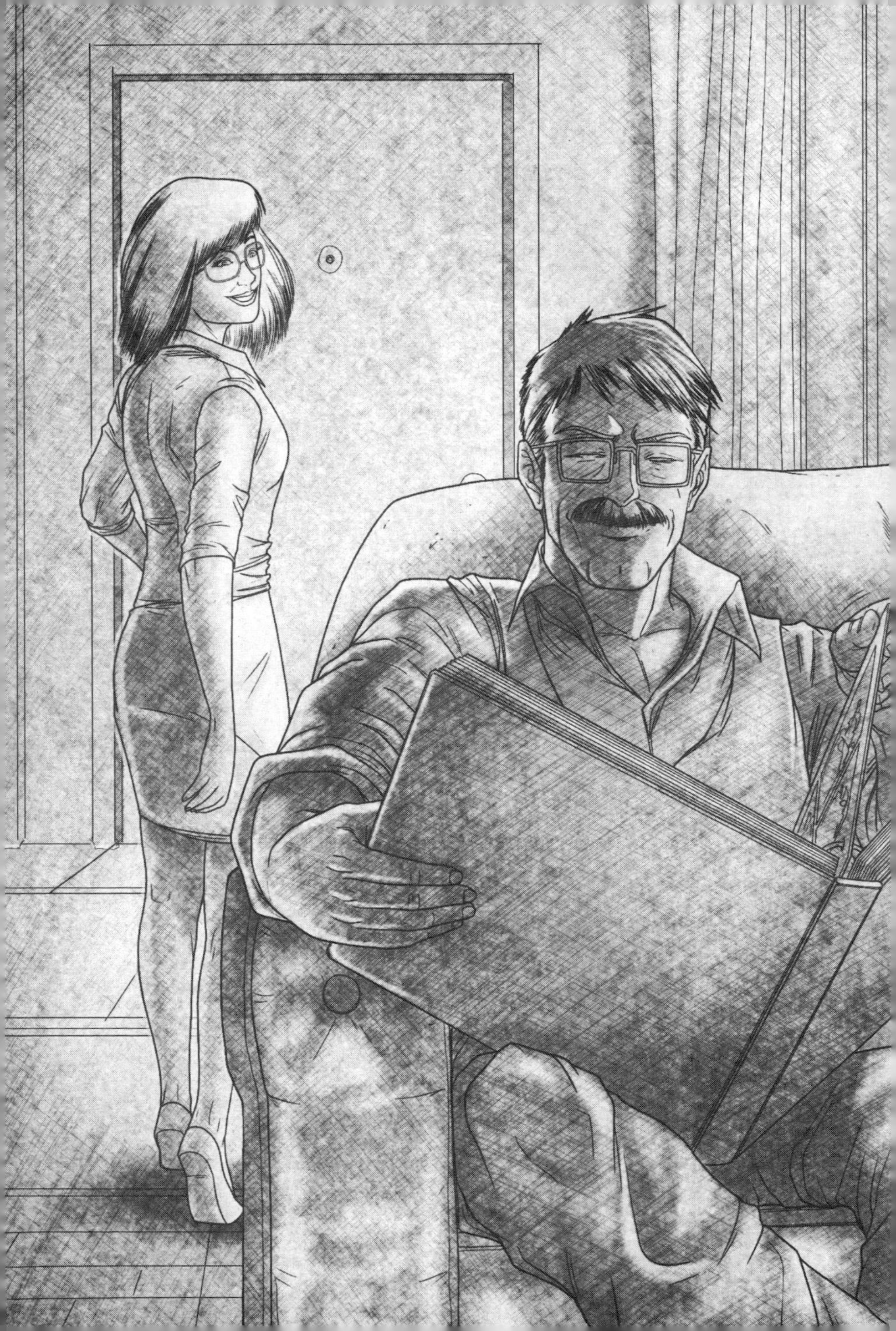

CHAPTER FOUR

A TEST OF WILL

It all began with a simple knock at the door. Barbara was entertaining her father, looking through a scrapbook of her Batman clippings. The rap at the front door caught her by surprise. When she opened it, the last thing she expected to see was the smiling face of one of Gotham City's most notorious criminals: the Joker.

Barbara was out of practice. She'd given up her life as Batgirl and therefore didn't react as quickly as she would have a year earlier. The Joker managed to fire off a shot from the gun in his hand. The bullet pierced Barbara's spine and sent her falling to the floor. When the pain finally subsided, she realized what had happened. She couldn't feel her legs. She was paralyzed from the waist down.

THE JOKER'S CRUELEST "PRANK" INVOLVED SHOOTING BARBARA GORDON IN AN ATTEMPT TO DRIVE COMMISSIONER JAMES GORDON INSANE.

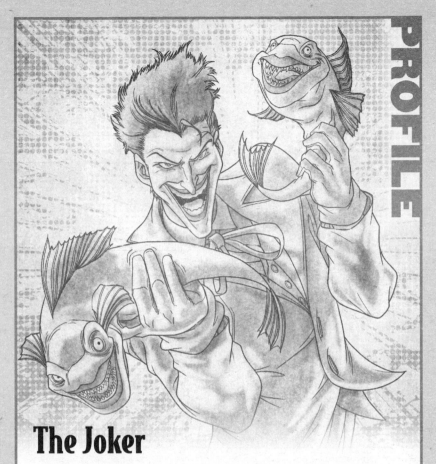

The Joker

He's Gotham City's Clown Prince of Crime: the smiling killer capable of unspeakable acts of evil. Presumably the leader of the notorious Red Hood Gang, the man who would be called the Joker once fell into a vat of chemicals. His skin was bleached white, his hair dyed green, and his lips became a permanent ruby red. Driven insane by the experience, he became obsessed with Batman and developed a sick sense of humor. Armed with his infamous Joker Venom, the super-villain is one of the most dangerous threats to Gotham City.

Although Batman found the Joker and brought him to justice, Barbara's life had once again been forever altered. She was full of an anger she'd never experienced. She had given her all for Gotham City, yet Gotham City had demanded more. But Barbara refused to act helpless. She began an experimental treatment that could possibly heal her spine by way of a technologically advanced spinal implant. As the doctors prepared for her surgery, Barbara threw herself into her own work. She began developing an artificial intelligence program based on her own brain scan. When completed, the algorithm would be able to predict crime before it happened. She could then become an "information broker" and send out operatives to fix any given situation from the comfort of her own home.

While at the doctor's office, Barbara met a new friend named Frankie Charles. Frankie shared Barbara's love of computers and athletics, and she also suffered from similar health problems. Frankie's

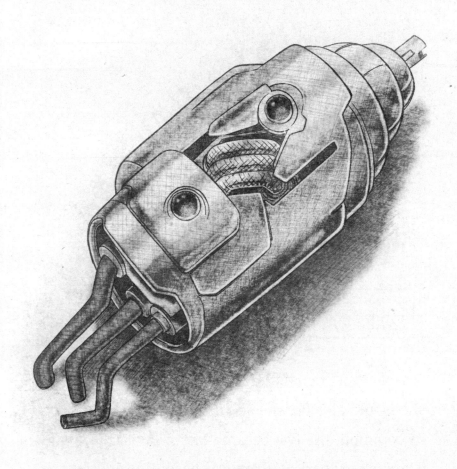

BARBARA GORDON'S SOPHISTICATED SPINAL IMPLANT.

EVEN WHILE BARBARA WAS PARALYZED FOR A TIME, SHE
CONTINUED HER PHYSICAL TRAINING WITH THE HELP OF HER
NEW FRIEND, FRANKIE.

muscles were rapidly deteriorating, and in a few years,
she would also be wheelchair-bound. With so much
in common, the two became fast friends. Even with
Frankie's support, Barbara was becoming angrier and
angrier with her situation. Her artificial intelligence
work became her priority, though Frankie warned her

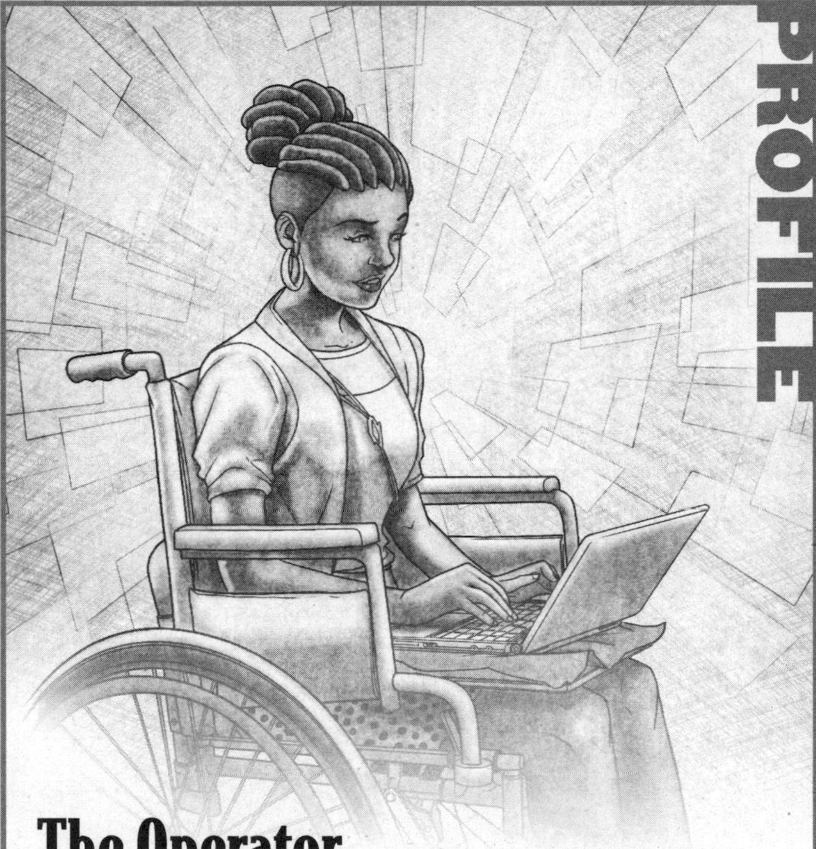
PROFILE

The Operator

Frankie Charles is a computer guru whose expertise rivals that of Barbara Gordon herself. She first met Barbara after being diagnosed with a disease that causes muscle deterioration. Despite her own struggles, Frankie became a bright light in Barbara's life. She helped the heroine fight off self-pity and anger during Barbara's recovery from a spinal injury. Frankie eventually discovered Barbara's secret life as Batgirl and adopted the role of the Operator, assisting Batgirl by hacking computers and feeding her vital information during her missions.

that the code she was developing could be extremely dangerous if it fell into the wrong hands.

Fortunately, Barbara soon underwent her experimental surgery, and it was a rousing success.

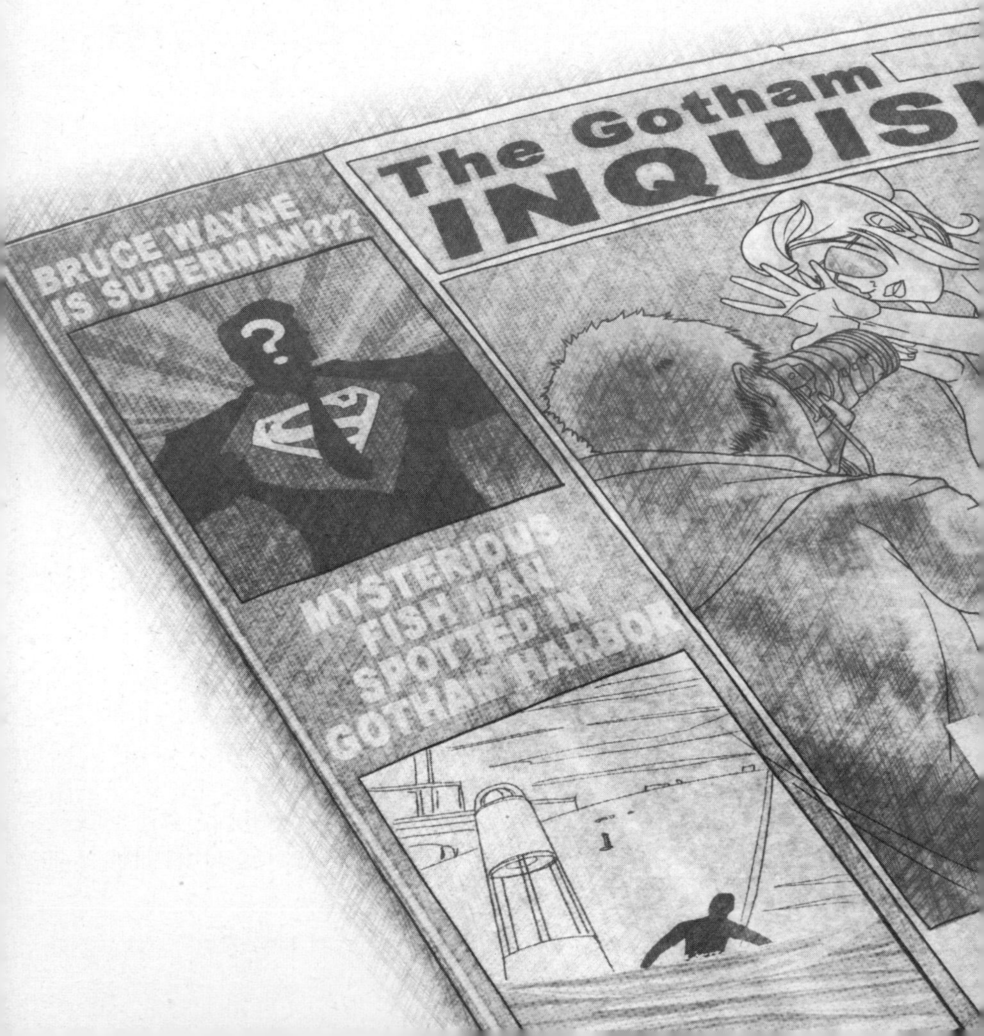
The Gotham
INQUIS
BRUCE WAYNE IS SUPERMAN???
MYSTERIOUS FISH MAN SPOTTED IN GOTHAM HARBOR

She was nicknamed the "Miracle Girl" and appeared on talk shows, receiving more than her fair share of press. Through the rough road of physical therapy, Barbara was getting back in fighting shape.

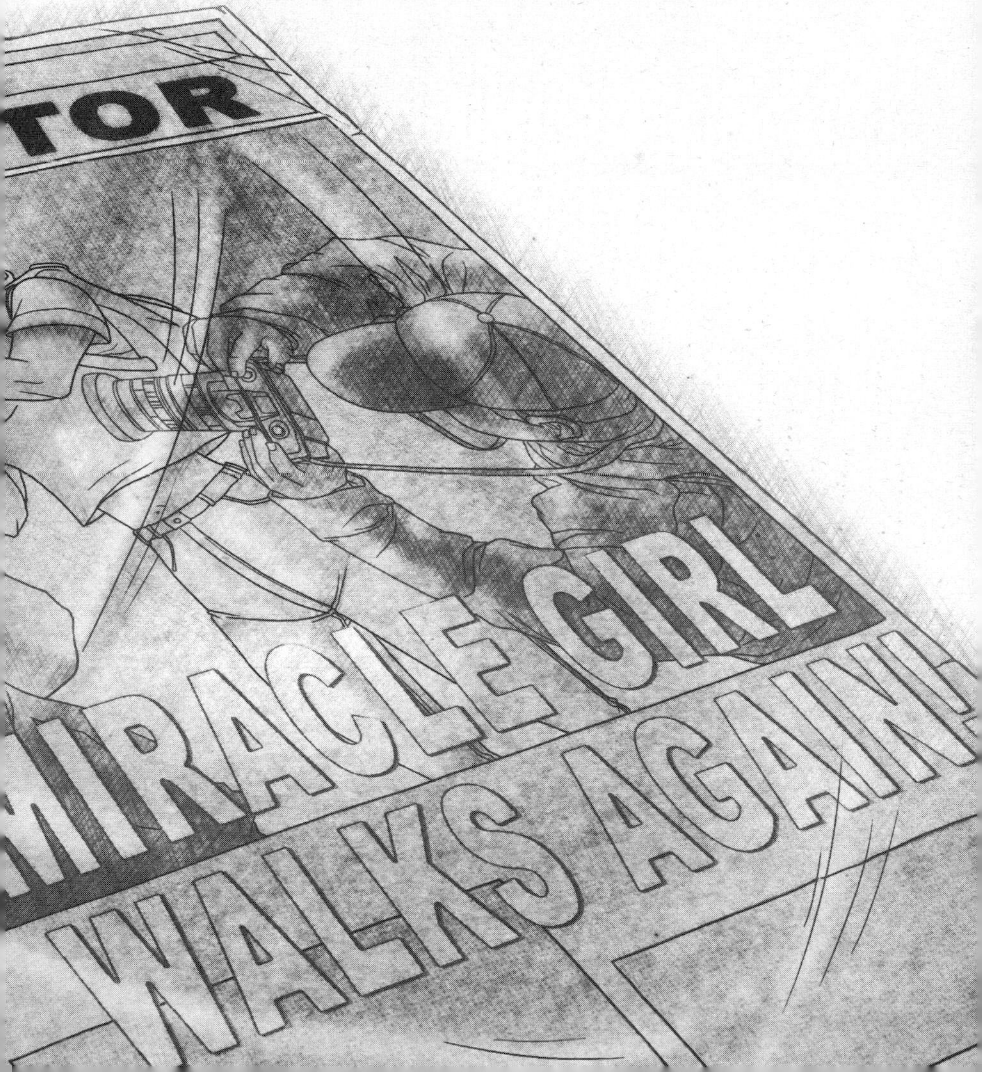
TOR
MIRACLE GIRL
WALKS AGAIN!

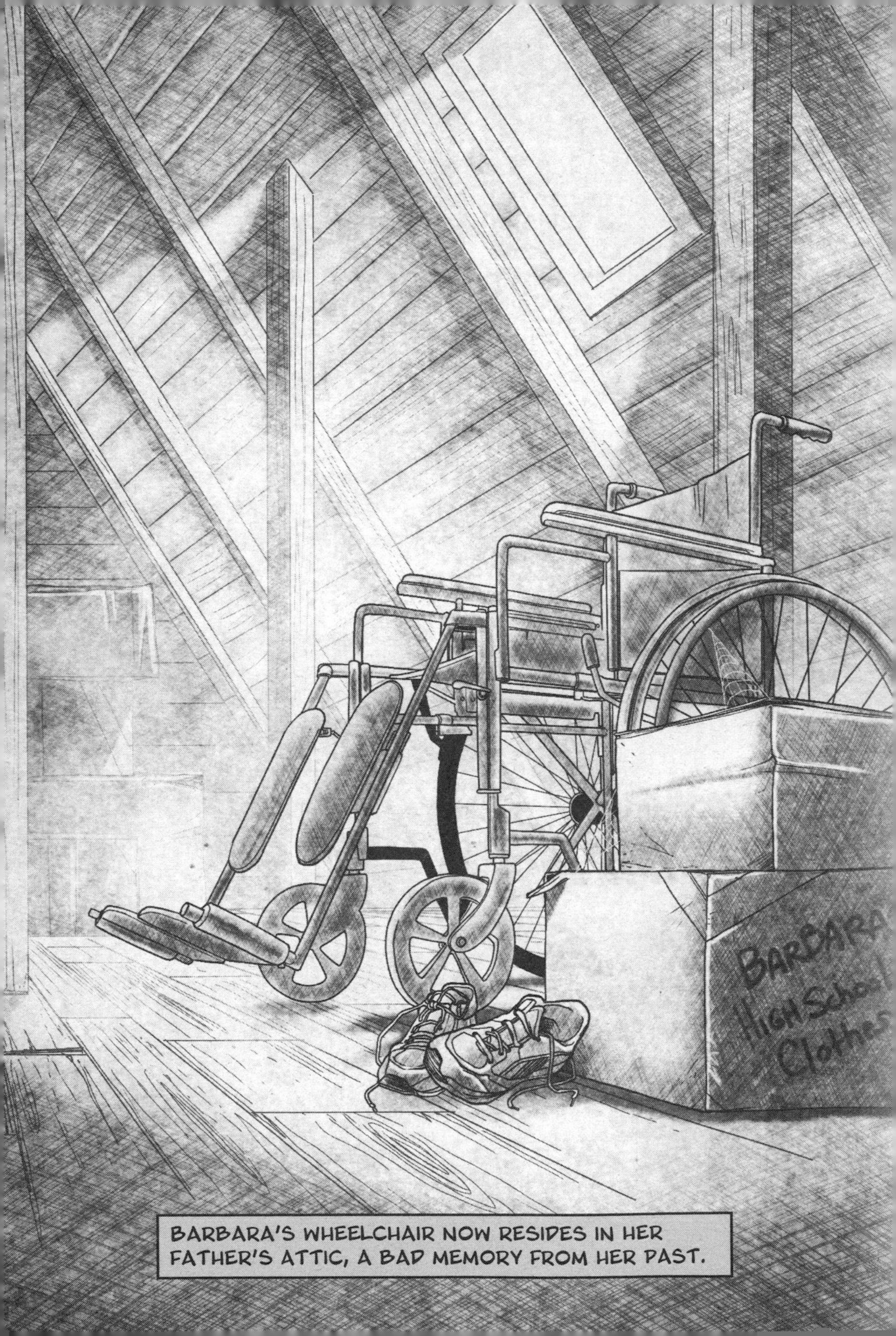
BARBARA
High School
Clothes
BARBARA'S WHEELCHAIR NOW RESIDES IN HER FATHER'S ATTIC, A BAD MEMORY FROM HER PAST.

However, a large part of her recovery was mental. Barbara realized she had to toughen up and not let making mistakes stop her from doing what she loved. She gave up on her risky artificial intelligence program and began to embrace her old life once again.

The true Barbara Gordon had returned. The only question that remained was: Would Batgirl's return soon follow?

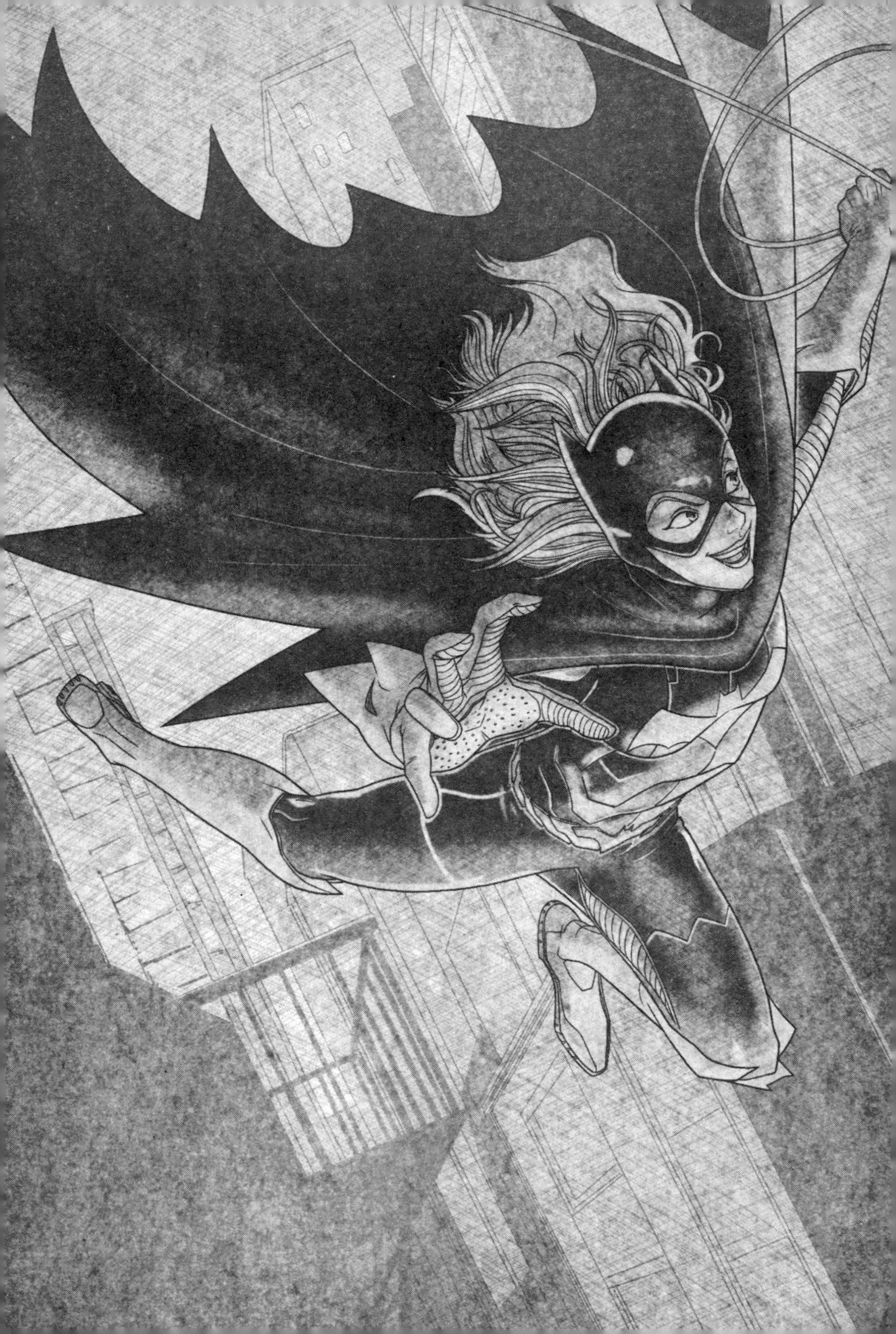

CHAPTER FIVE

RETURN TO ACTION

She had retaught herself to walk. Now it was time to learn once again how to fly. Barbara Gordon was no longer content to sit on the sidelines—it was time to become Batgirl again. She was determined to become a new kind of crime fighter. This time around, she would be smarter, tougher, and not let lunatics like the Joker stand in her way.

The first order of business was the costume. Barbara's original Batgirl suit had offered little protection from the many dangers of Gotham City.

Her new costume came as a gift from Batman and was just as high tech as the Batsuit worn by the Dark Knight himself. The suit included protective yet

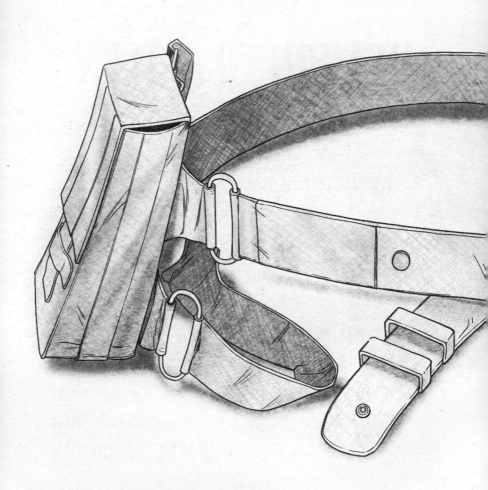

lightweight body armor, yellow boots and gloves, a
fully equipped and updated Utility Belt, a purple and
black cape, and most important, an armored cowl.

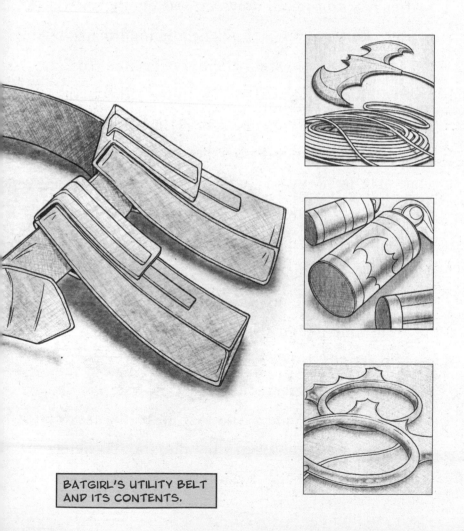

BATGIRL'S UTILITY BELT
AND ITS CONTENTS.

A simple bullet wouldn't catch Barbara unguarded again. This time, her body would be prepared for anything.

Her peace of mind, however, was another battle entirely. Barbara was still plagued by nightmares of the Joker's home invasion. She was hesitant to act on her instincts, and that sometimes allowed her enemies to escape in a fight. But Barbara desperately wanted to move on with her life. She found a new apartment in Gotham City's Cherry Hill district and moved in with a roommate named Alysia Yeoh, a self-proclaimed political activist. The two became good friends, even though Alysia became suspicious of Barbara's many late nights away from home.

Meanwhile, Batgirl continued to adjust to a life back in action. Her first encounter with the Mirror, a psychotic murderer with a long hit list, was the true test to determine if she was up to the task of protecting Gotham again. It was the challenge she needed to finally regain her self-confidence.

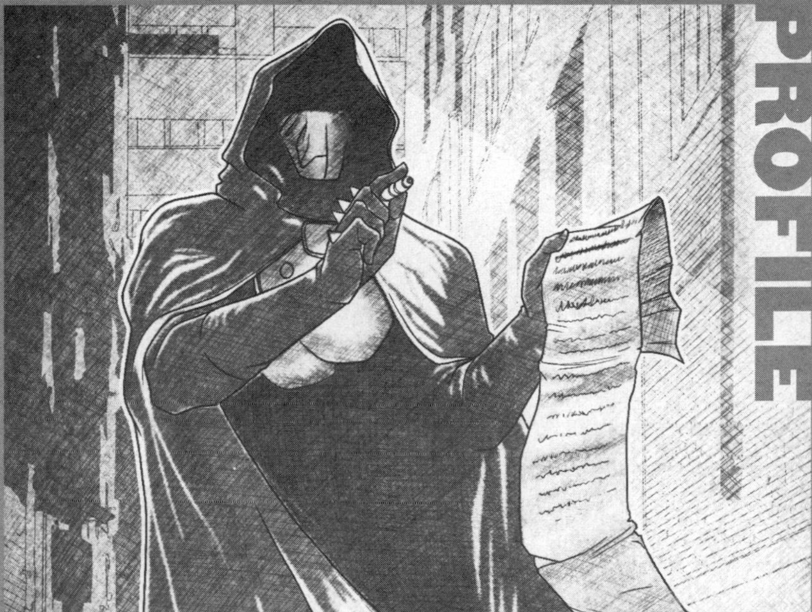
PROFILE

The Mirror

Like most super-villains, Jonathan Mills's life is full of tragedy. He originally worked for the DEA (Drug Enforcement Administration) and was one of the best agents in the field. However, when a criminal killed his family, he became obsessed with anyone who, like him, survived impossible odds. Donning the costume of the Mirror, Mills made a list of those individuals and plotted to kill them one by one, until Batgirl intervened and ended his criminal campaign.

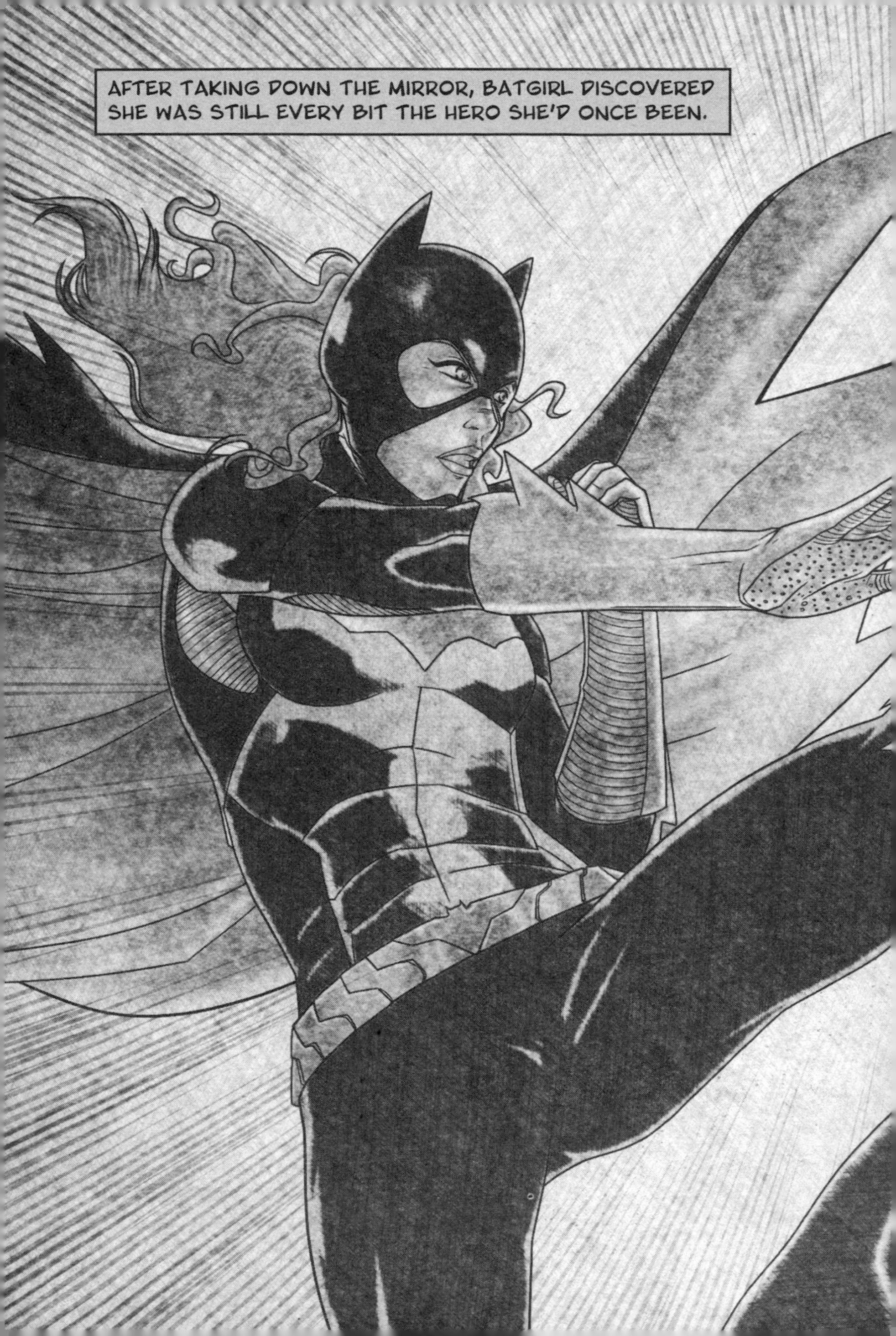
AFTER TAKING DOWN THE MIRROR, BATGIRL DISCOVERED SHE WAS STILL EVERY BIT THE HERO SHE'D ONCE BEEN.

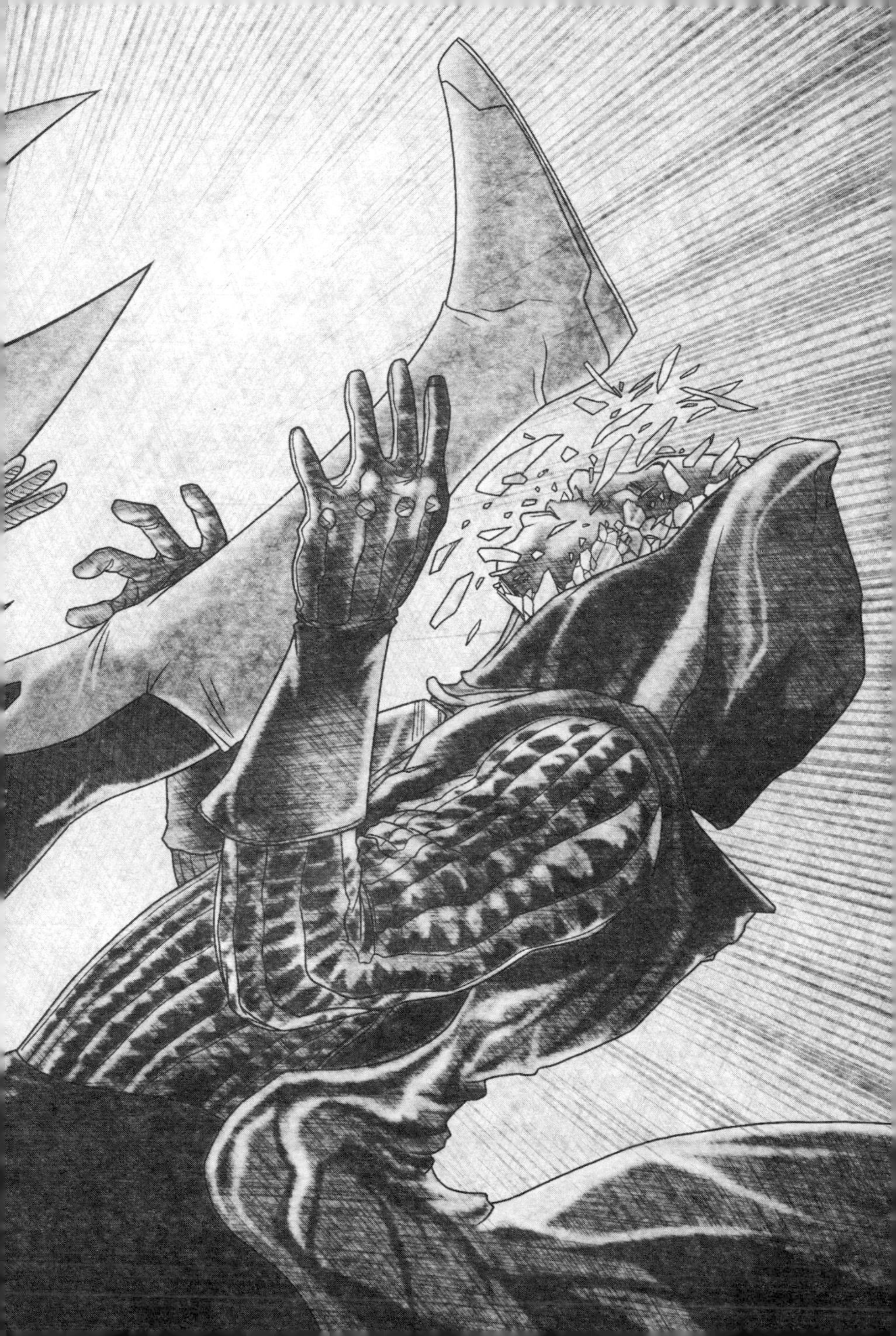

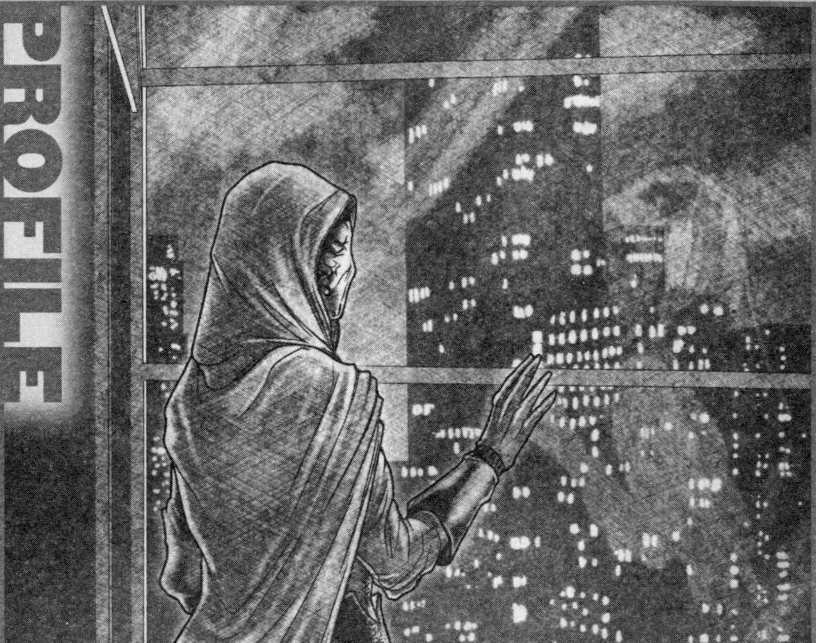
PROFILE

Knightfall

When she was young, Charise Carnes watched with horror as her boyfriend murdered her family. She swore revenge against the killer, but instead of reporting him to the police, Charise took the blame for her family's death. After being imprisoned in Arkham Asylum for the Criminally Insane, Charise was released. She then enacted her plan by kidnapping her ex-boyfriend. She would have finally killed her family's murderer if not for Batgirl's timely intervention.

Barbara defeated the twisted villain, realizing she was back in control of her life and stronger than ever.

The Mirror wasn't the only new threat to cross Batgirl's path. Soon she met Gretel, a superhuman with the ability to control the minds of men. Batgirl learned that Gretel's true identity was Lisly Bonner, a journalist injured while going undercover to spy on a known criminal. Her near-death experience had caused her to gain mind control powers, and she almost succeeded in overcoming the strong will of Bruce Wayne. Fortunately, Batgirl and Batman teamed up and managed to defeat her.

Batgirl was back in the swing of things. While her new enemies had been challenging, all would pale in comparison to the woman called Knightfall. To the general public, Charise Carnes was a philanthropist trying to improve the Cherry Hill neighborhood. However, Batgirl saw through Charise's act and discovered she was a criminal obsessed with killing all other criminals. Despite Batgirl's repeated attempts to bring Knightfall to justice, the villain was only defeated when she grew too ambitious. Knightfall hired many of Batgirl's enemies to team up against her. Batgirl responded in kind, employing many Super Heroes to battle Knightfall's operatives, while she herself took Charise down.

The drama in Barbara Gordon's life was not limited to the kind brought on by masked strangers. Her mother, Barbara Kean Gordon, finally returned to Gotham City and attempted to reconcile with her daughter after such a long time with no contact. Meanwhile, Batgirl's brother James Gordon Jr. wanted nothing more than to keep his family apart. During a conflict with Batgirl, he plunged into a river. Batgirl thought her brother was dead, only to discover later that he had survived the encounter. James Jr. would go on to aid the Suicide Squad, a secret government task force, before returning to Gotham City to cause more trouble. The whole ordeal proved to be too much for Barbara Kean, and

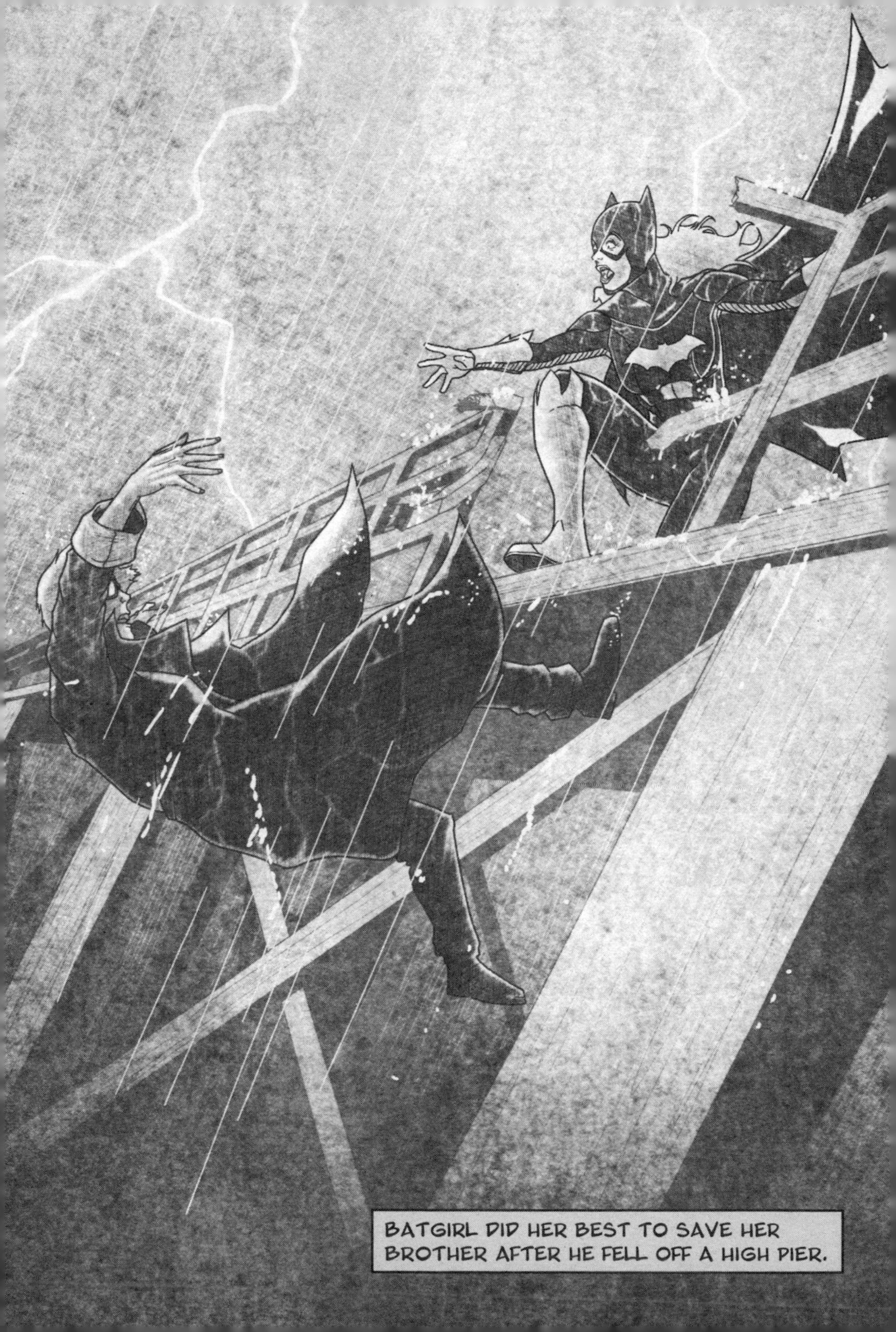
BATGIRL DID HER BEST TO SAVE HER BROTHER AFTER HE FELL OFF A HIGH PIER.

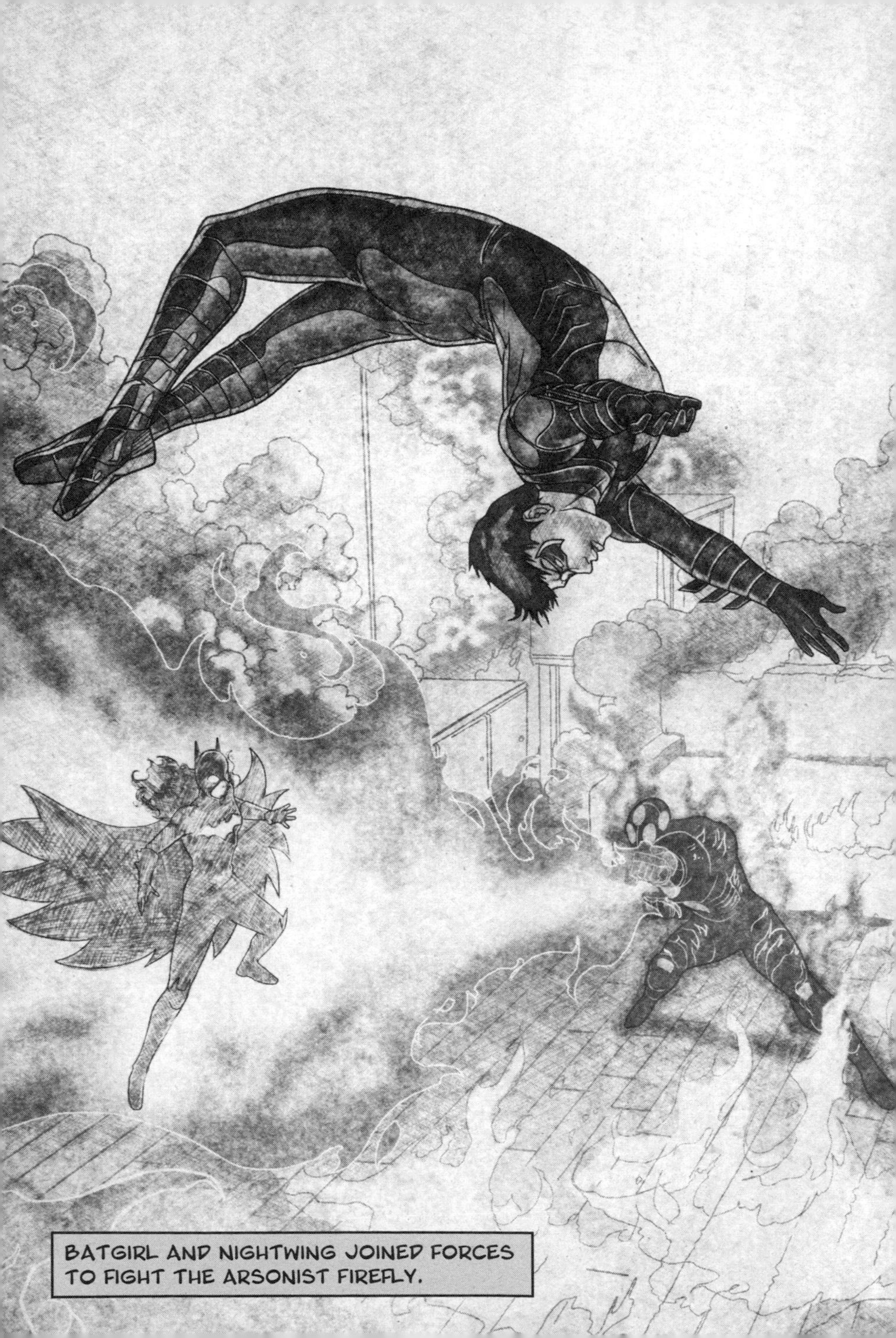
BATGIRL AND NIGHTWING JOINED FORCES TO FIGHT THE ARSONIST FIREFLY.

she soon left Gotham City for good.

Batgirl had reestablished herself as a heroine to be reckoned with. She faced down the likes of high-profile villains such as the pyromaniac Firefly and the demented, telekinetic Ventriloquist. But she didn't fight her war alone. Aside from team-ups with heroes like Batman and Nightwing, Batgirl also found friends in the strangest corners of Gotham City— friends who would help shape her into a respected hero not only in her hometown, but also throughout the entire Super Hero community.

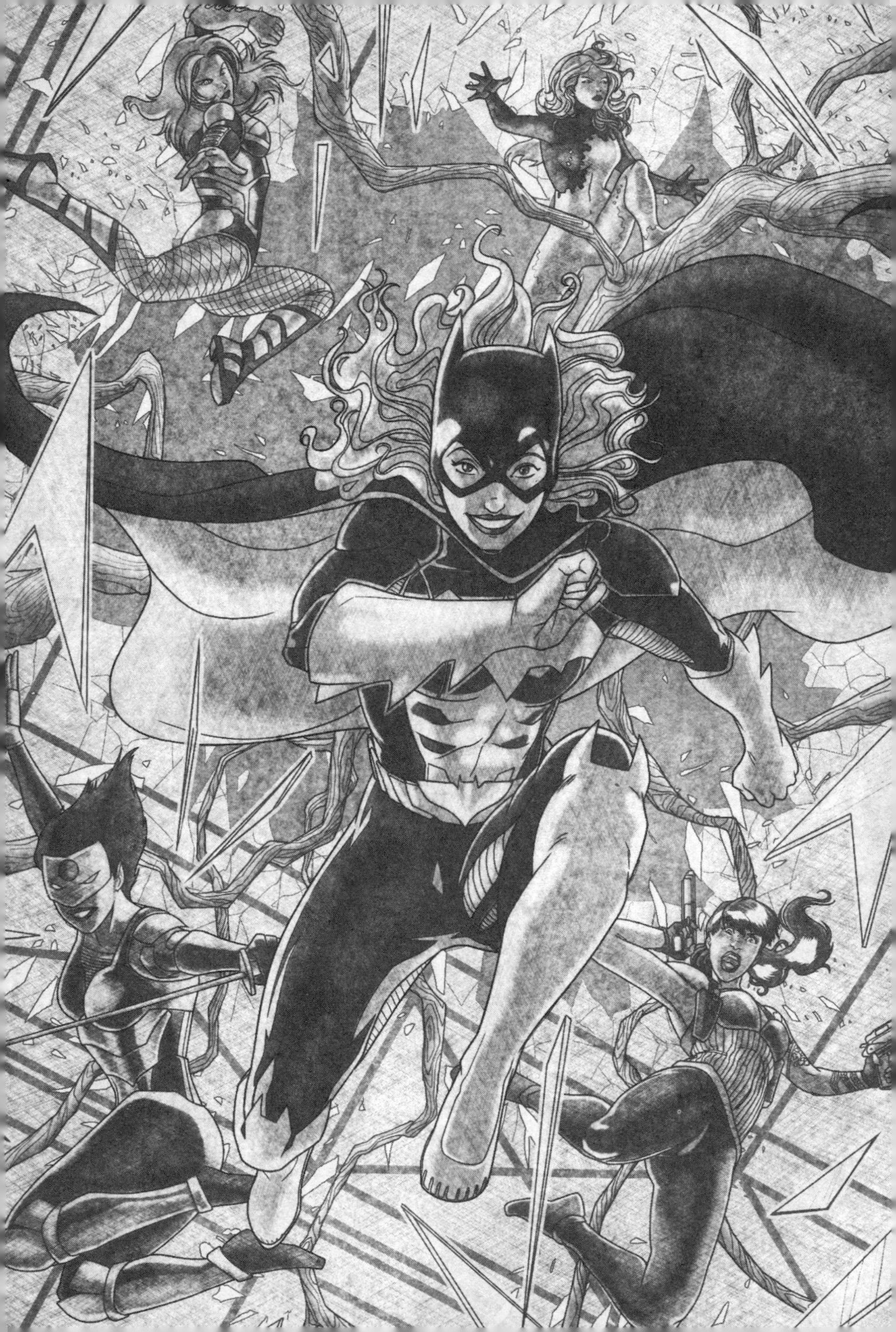

CHAPTER SIX

THE BIRDS OF PREY

Batman has never been comfortable in a team environment. Despite working with multiple partners over the years and even serving on the Justice League, a team of the world's greatest Super Heroes, Batman prefers working alone. Like her mentor, Batgirl is an effective lone agent. And while she normally relishes Batman's example, when it comes to being a team player, the two don't quite see eye to eye.

After Barbara took on the identity of Batgirl for

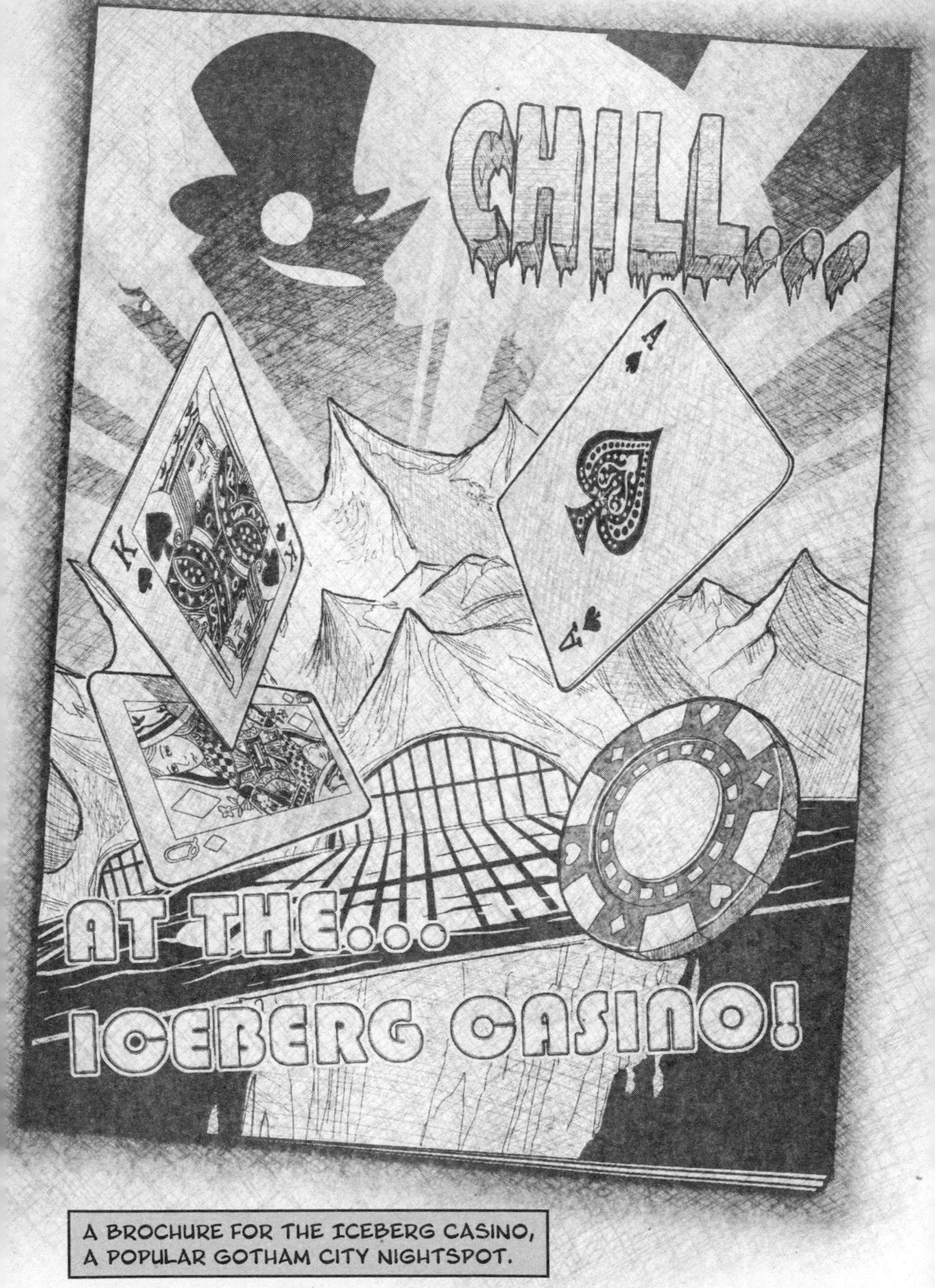
CHILL....
AT THE...
ICEBERG CASINO!

A BROCHURE FOR THE ICEBERG CASINO,
A POPULAR GOTHAM CITY NIGHTSPOT.

the second time, one of her missions led her to the Iceberg Casino floating in Gotham Bay. The infamous casino was a guilty pleasure of Gotham City's rich and famous. It was a place where high society could rub elbows with the criminal element. The floating nightclub was owned by Oswald Cobblepot, otherwise known as Batman's longtime enemy, the Penguin.

The Penguin was known for making many illegal deals, running his criminal operations in back rooms while he presented himself as an honest businessman to the public. One such deal was the sale of a highly dangerous bomb—and Batgirl was on a mission to shut it down. On the night the Penguin planned to sell his illegal device, Batgirl burst through the casino's skylight. She was instantly confronted by several of the Penguin's henchwomen. The women were highly skilled fighters, each named after a bird to keep with the Penguin's favorite theme. However, in the mix was an undercover vigilante who went by the code name Black Canary.

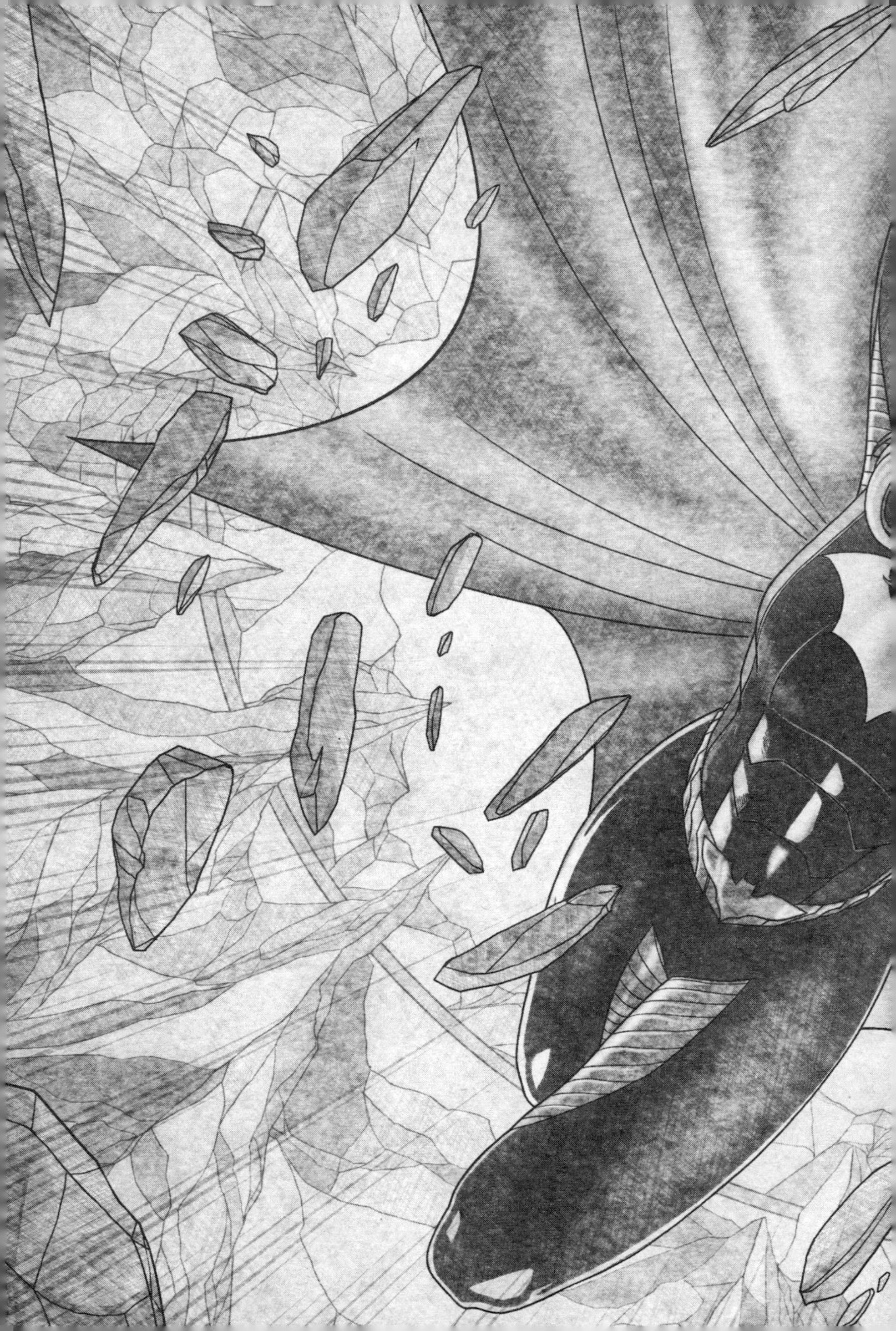

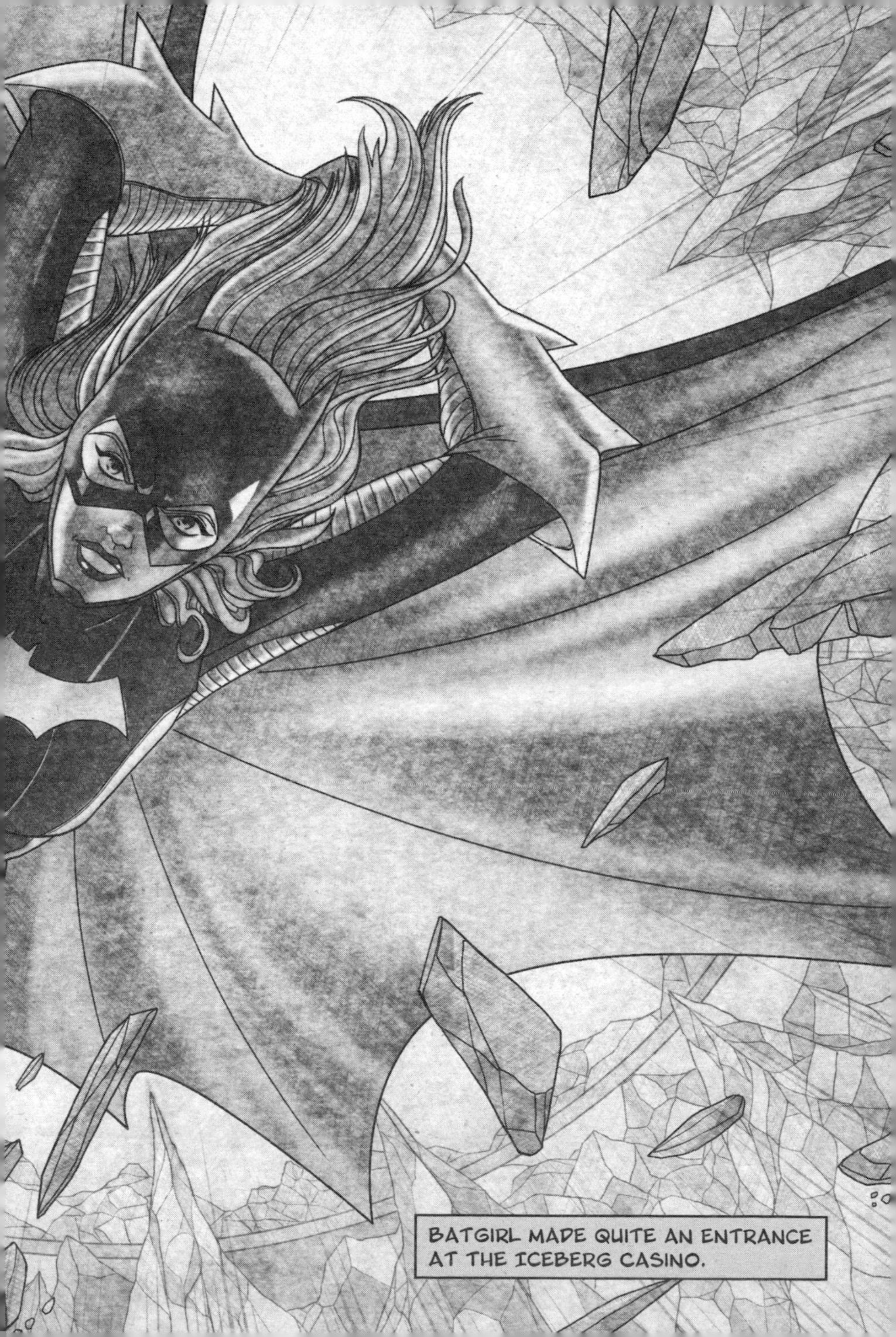
BATGIRL MADE QUITE AN ENTRANCE AT THE ICEBERG CASINO.

THE PENGUIN AND HIS TWO FORMER EMPLOYEES, BLACK CANARY AND STARLING.

Black Canary was a former government agent who had gone rogue, deciding to fight crime in her own way. She had joined the Penguin's crew a week earlier to shut down the very deal Batgirl was there to end. While working with the Penguin's employees, Canary had befriended Evelyn Crawford, an expert fighter who went by the name Starling.

When Batgirl first leapt onto the scene, the women were unaware they were all trying to accomplish the same goal. Batgirl quickly disarmed Starling, but Black Canary proved much more of a challenge. The two seemed evenly matched, trading punch for punch, kick for kick. Finally, when they had a moment away from prying ears, Canary managed to whisper to Batgirl that she was an undercover agent. Something in her voice told Batgirl to trust this mysterious new ally, and the two set out to end the operation together. Batgirl went after the Penguin, while Black Canary went after his customer.

The surprise spooked the Penguin's would-be

buyer. He raced away in a speedboat, but Black Canary didn't seem fazed. She simply put her hands to her mouth and released a sonic scream from her lips. The Canary Cry shattered the criminal's boat, allowing time for Canary to swim and apprehend him.

Batgirl had more of a challenge on her end. Starling surprised her and held her at gunpoint in front of the Penguin. When Black Canary arrived, she managed to convince her friend that she and Batgirl were on the side of justice. Starling joined the two heroines, escaping into the night. While Batgirl thought their partnership was over that evening, Black Canary had other plans. Canary was once again working with a team for the greater good, and she liked these new allies; she could get used to working with these fellow Birds of Prey.

Black Canary and Starling began working together on missions, and Batgirl found herself drawn to their adventures. Canary soon recruited two new members to their Birds of Prey team: the martial arts expert

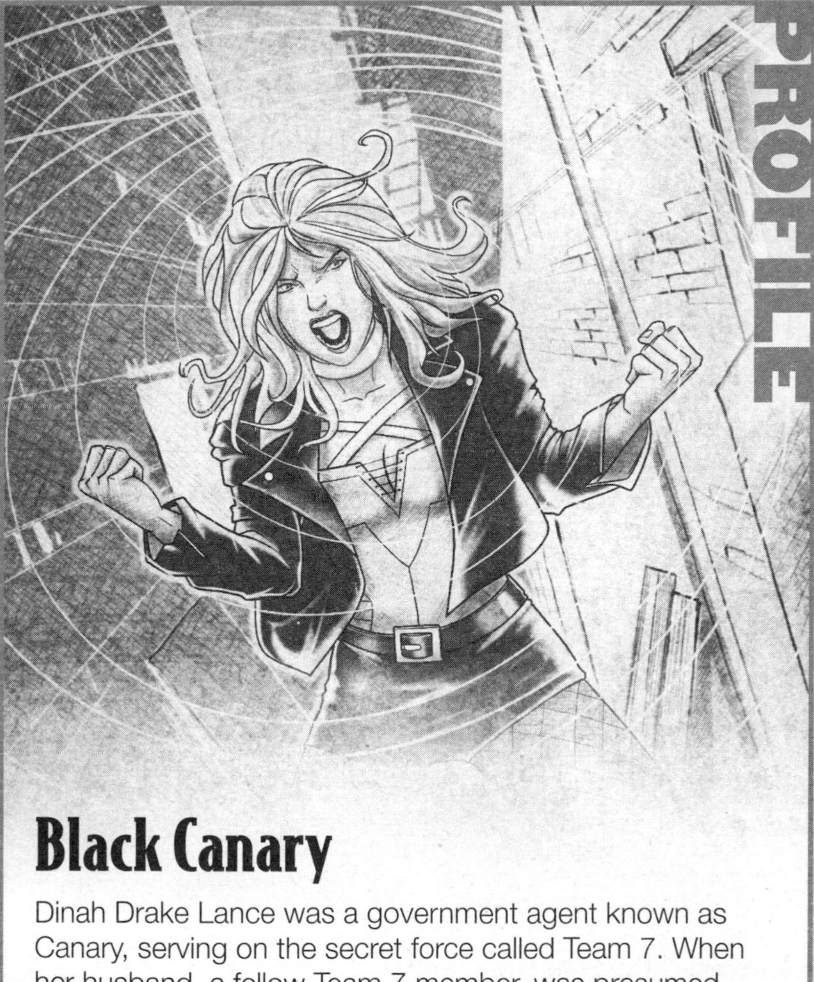
PROFILE

Black Canary

Dinah Drake Lance was a government agent known as Canary, serving on the secret force called Team 7. When her husband, a fellow Team 7 member, was presumed killed during a disastrous mission, Dinah went rogue. She quit the team and changed her moniker to Black Canary. She later became a founding member of the Birds of Prey, and in the process, she became one of Batgirl's most trusted friends. Dinah is also known to use her tremendous voice as lead singer for the popular band also called Black Canary.

Katana and the notorious plant-controlling supervillain Poison Ivy. Batgirl saw the potential danger in these choices, but the optimist in her believed that Katana could curb her violent tendencies and that Poison Ivy was capable of turning over a new leaf.

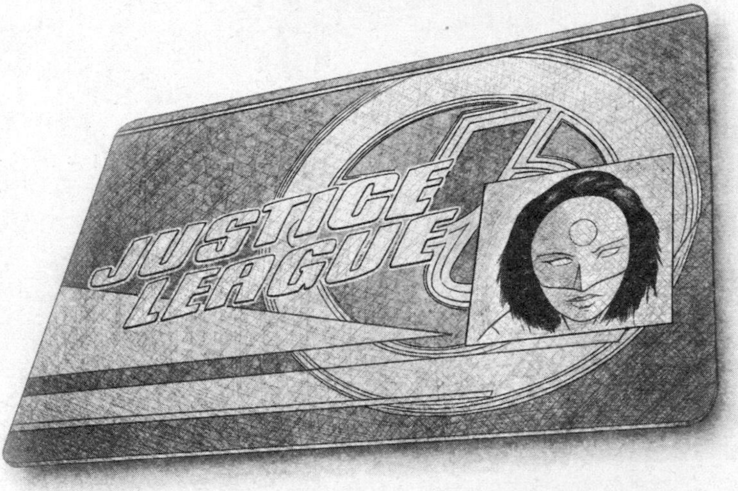
JUSTICE LEAGUE

KATANA HAS SERVED ON THE BIRDS OF PREY, THE JUSTICE LEAGUE OF AMERICA, AND THE TASK FORCE CALLED THE SUICIDE SQUAD.

Katana proved to be a noble warrior and valued ally. However, Poison Ivy didn't work out quite as well.

It wasn't long before Ivy turned on her teammates, proving her true nature. To make matters worse, Katana soon left the team to pursue personal matters.

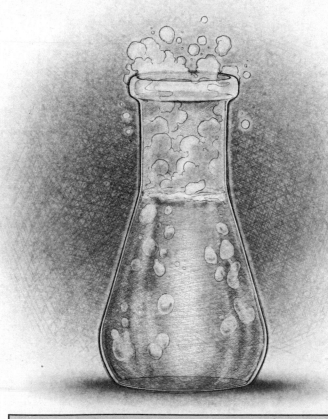

A VIAL OF THE CHEMICALS THAT GAVE POISON IVY HER PLANT-CONTROLLING POWERS IN A LAB ACCIDENT AT WAYNE ENTERPRISES.

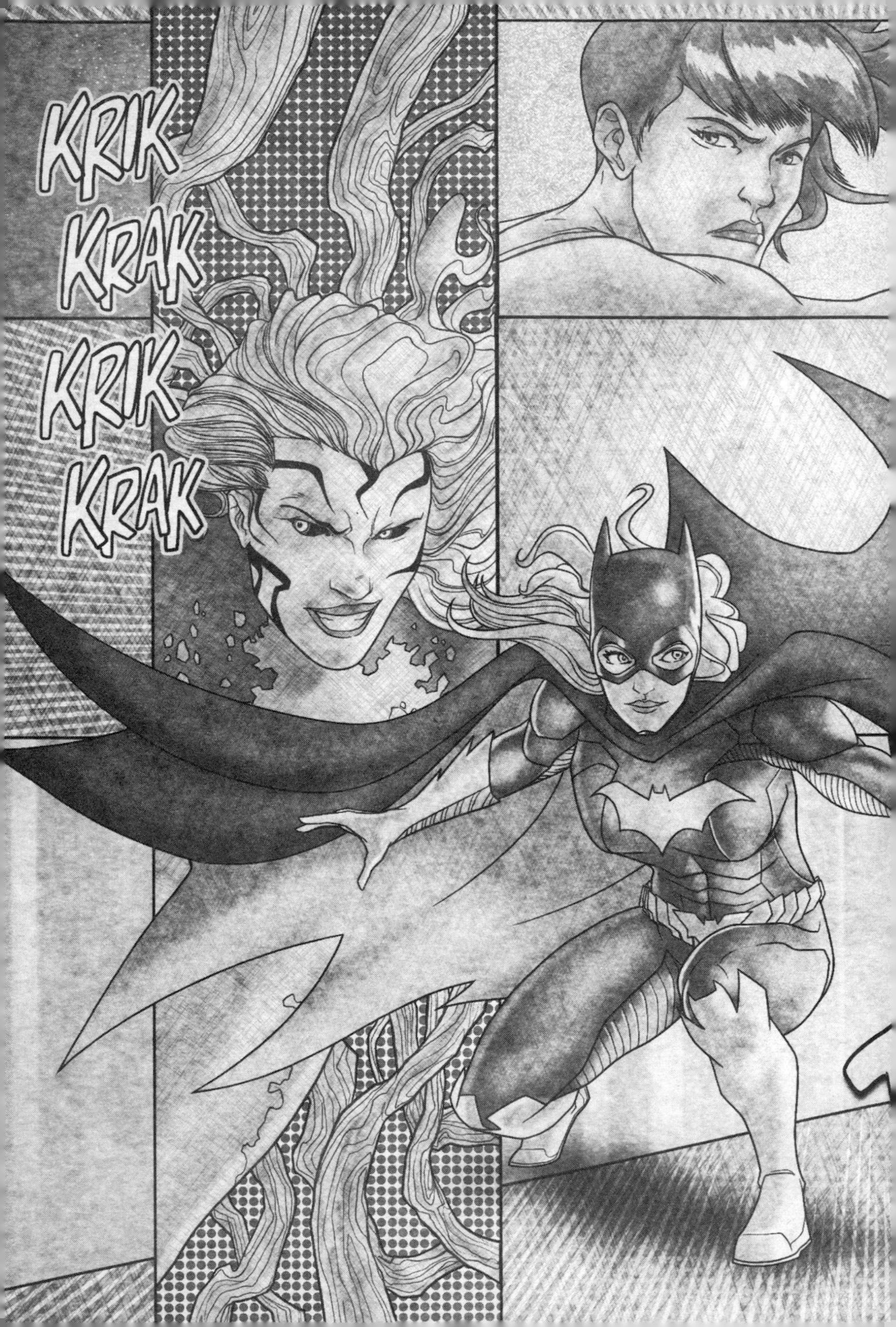
KRIK
KRAK
KRIK
KRAK

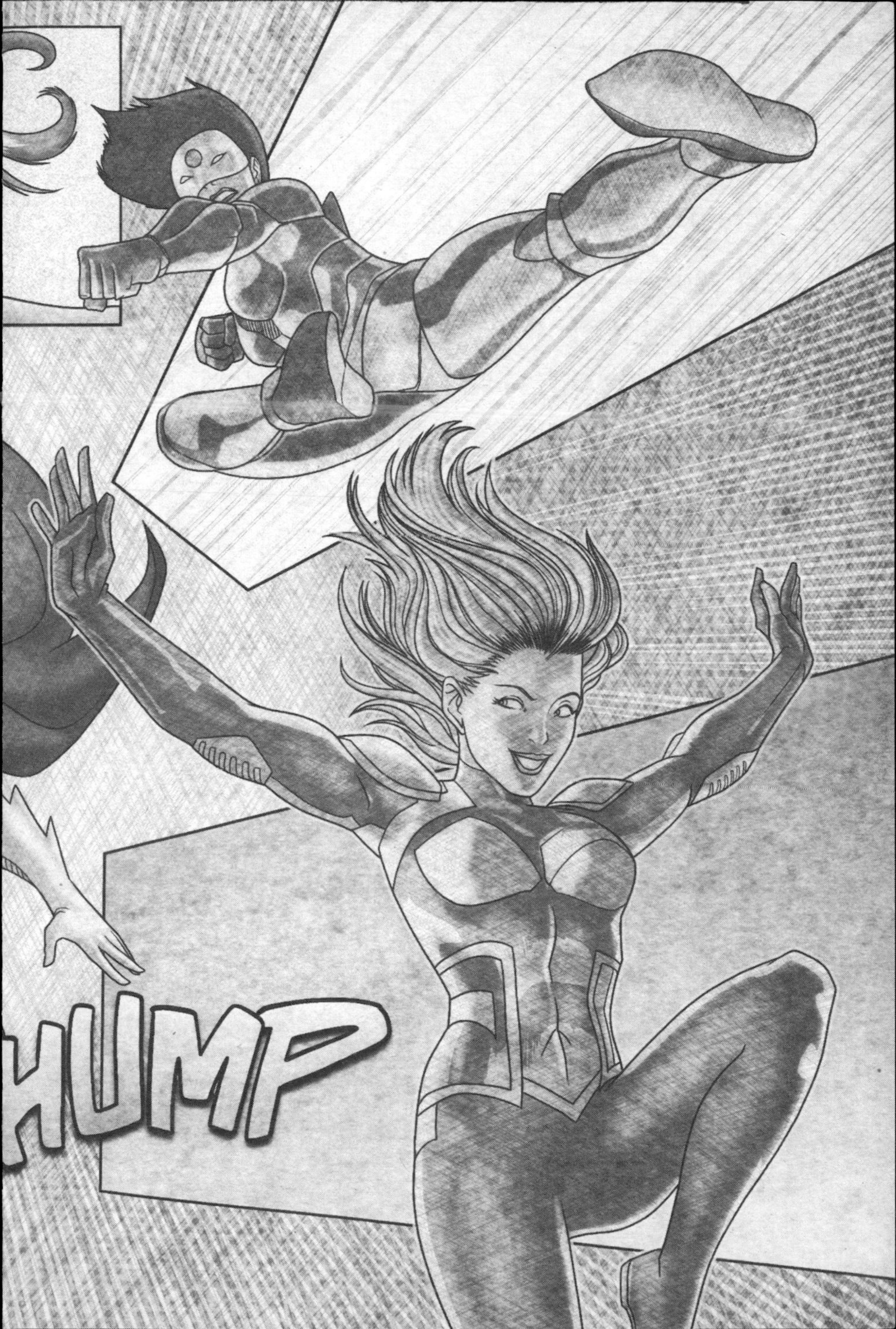
HUMP

To fill the void created in their absence, Batgirl recruited new member and reformed assassin Strix. Then the rather insistent telekinetic hero Condor talked his way onto the team. But before the Birds could fully adjust to their new members, there proved to be yet another traitor in their midst.

When the Birds of Prey found themselves up against the powerful villain Mr. Freeze, Starling revealed that she had been secretly working for Freeze for quite some time. She even chose to help the cold criminal fight against her former friends rather than prove her allegiance to the Birds. While Black Canary, Batgirl, Condor, and Strix escaped the fight with their lives, Starling made a clean getaway as well, earning the wrath of her former allies in the process.

After many valiant battles, the Birds decided to go their separate ways for a time. They had accomplished a lot during their limited tenure, but it was never enough for Batgirl.

PROFILE

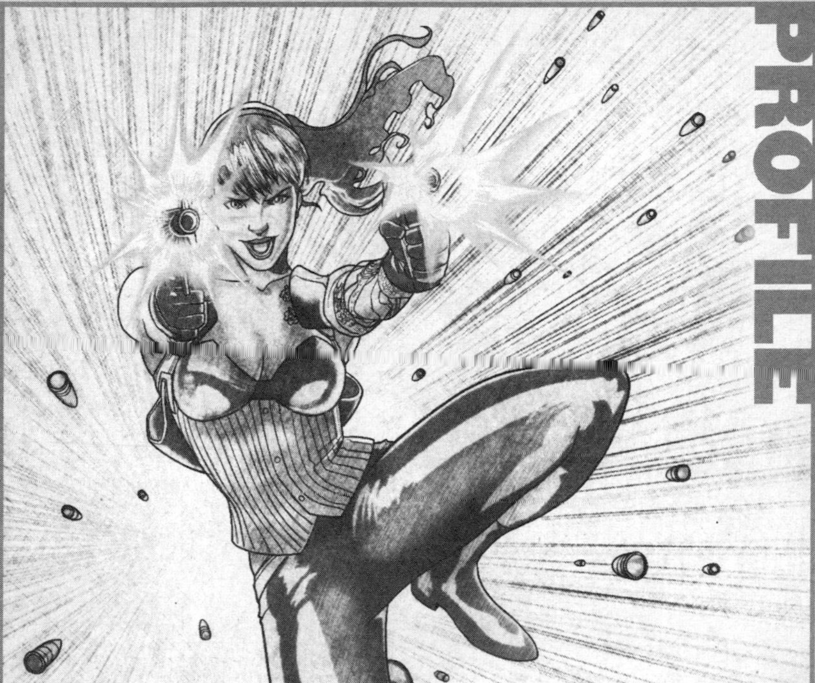

Starling

Evelyn Crawford had a difficult past that introduced her to many criminals and otherwise sketchy acquaintances. These people would become her future clients when she adopted the life of a freelance fighter. Starling has worked for the Penguin, government agent Amanda Waller, and even Mr. Freeze. It was her loyalty to Mr. Freeze that caused her to betray her teammates in the Birds of Prey. In an instant, Starling went from being one of Batgirl's most trusted allies to one of her most bitter enemies.

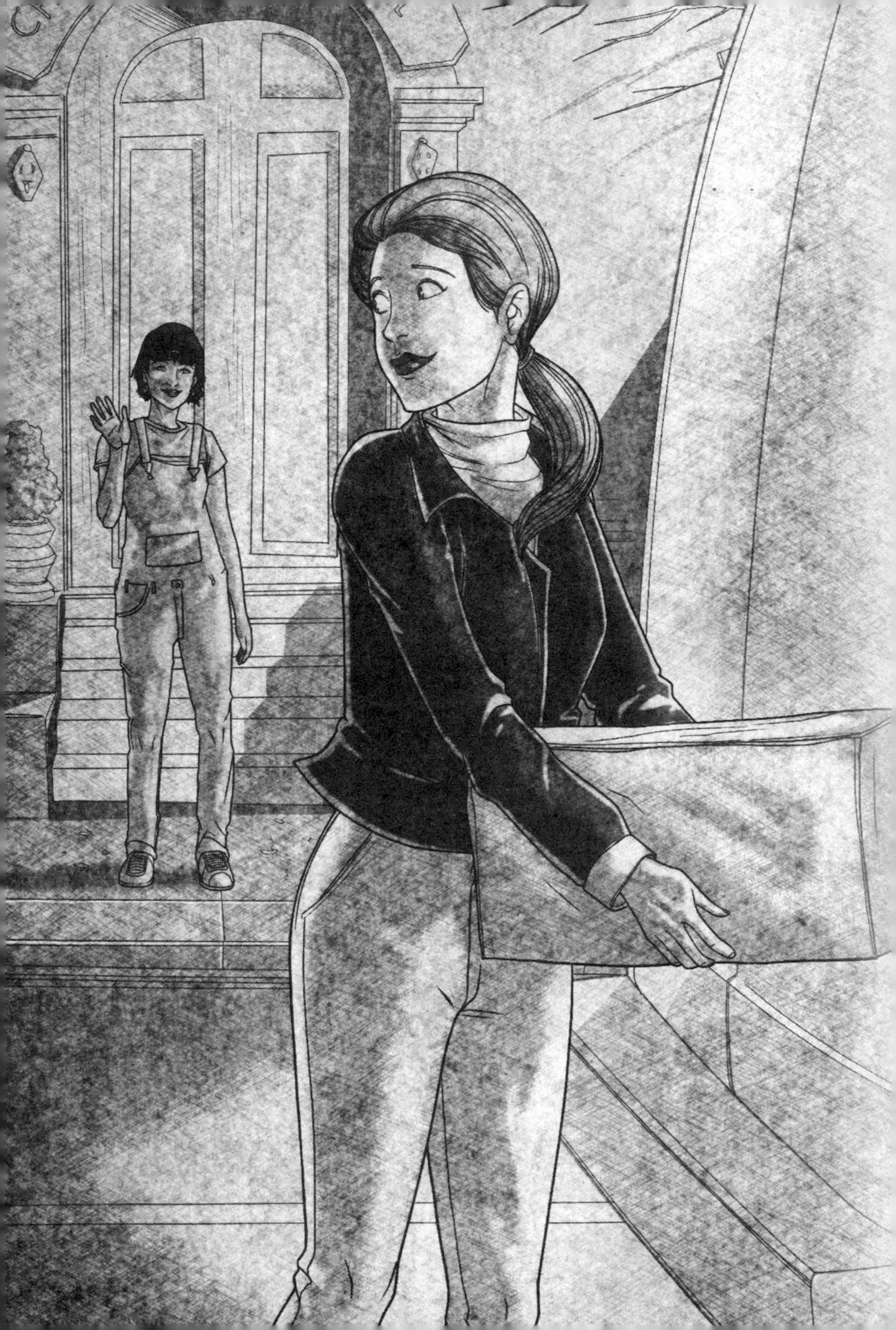

As long as she lived in Gotham City, Barbara couldn't help but feel like a child still living at home with her parents. She was firmly in the shadow of the Dark Knight and her father, as well as continually haunted by the tragedies that laced her past. It was time for her to leave Cherry Hill and her old life behind. She was ready for a fresh start—for both Barbara Gordon and Batgirl.

BARBARA BIDS FAREWELL TO HER ROOMMATE, ALYSIA.

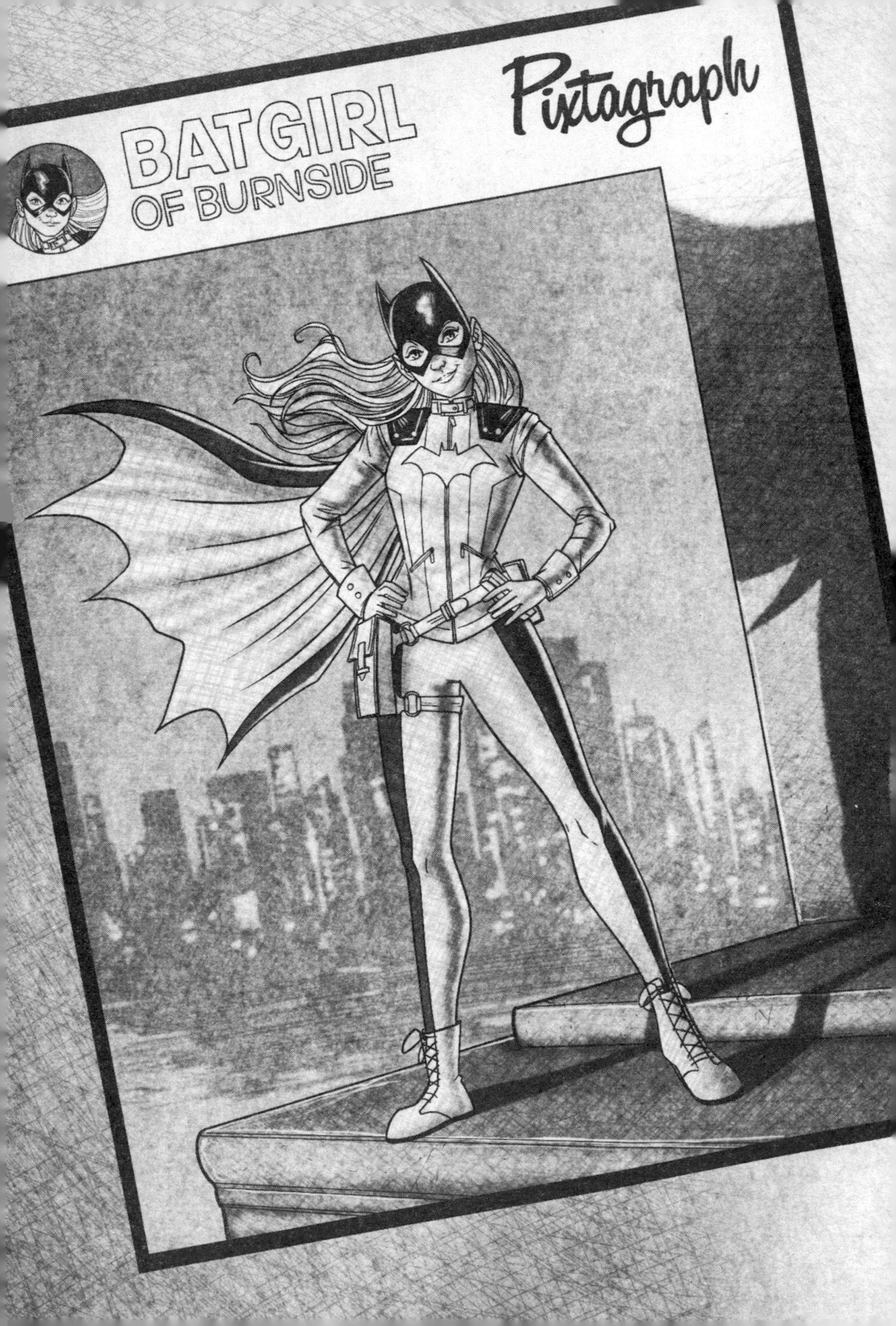
Pixtagraph
BATGIRL
OF BURNSIDE

CHAPTER SEVEN

THE BATGIRL OF BURNSIDE

All her life, Barbara Gordon had been trying to mimic someone else. First, she tried to live up to her father's good example. Then she patterned her secret life after that of Batman. It was time for Batgirl to venture out into the world alone and find out just what kind of woman she truly was. To do that, she had to leave Gotham City's Cherry Hill neighborhood in favor of one of the town's most popular and trendy boroughs, Burnside.

Barbara's friend Frankie Charles lived in this part of town on a quiet, tree-lined street. She and Barbara had maintained their friendship ever since meeting at the doctor's office years ago. It only made sense that

Batgirl @Batgirl
Thanks for the heads up about a certain villain's return, Burnside... thanks to you guys, that moth just got squashed!

Batgirl @Batgirl reposted
@Batgirl_Fan26 Batgirl @Batgirl is my HERO—and she seems way more fun to hang out with than Batman. #tightenupdude

Batgirl @Batgirl
@Operator, wanna pick up the popcorn for our movie night? I have the DVDs ready!

BATGIRL USES HER SMARTPHONE TO KEEP IN DIRECT CONTACT WITH THE PEOPLE OF BURNSIDE.

Frankie welcomed her with open arms as her new roommate. Soon, Black Canary paid Barbara a visit to break the news that her old home had burned down, including the storage area where Batgirl had kept her costume and gear. But Barbara wasn't about to let a setback ruin her life as Batgirl a second time. Instead, she crafted a new, handmade Batsuit. The Utility Belt on this costume held one of her most important new tools in fighting crime: her cell phone.

No longer living in Batman's shadow, Batgirl was ready to fight crime her way. That meant using social media for research and to make her presence in Burnside known. Fans could send her information or clues that would help her in a case—a far cry from the loner activities of Gotham City's Dark Knight.

While her career as Batgirl began to truly take off, Barbara entered graduate school. There, she found a wealth of new friends, including robotics expert Qadir Ali. Qadir became Batgirl's go-to tech guy, building tools for her arsenal such as a new grappling gun.

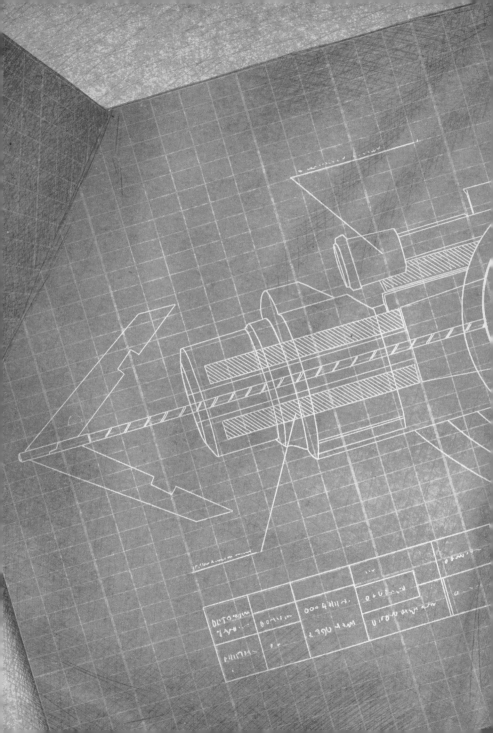

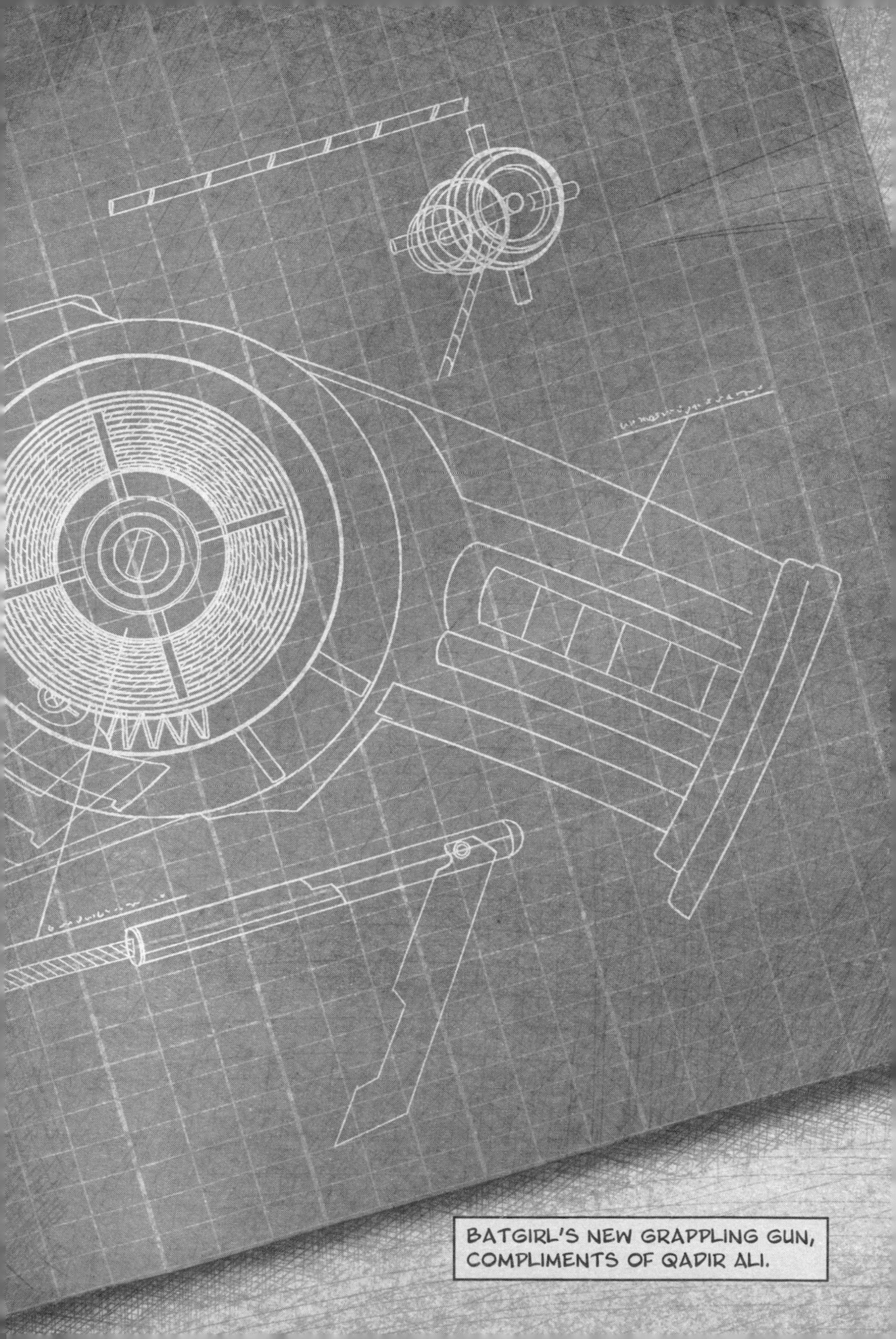
BATGIRL'S NEW GRAPPLING GUN, COMPLIMENTS OF QADIR ALI.

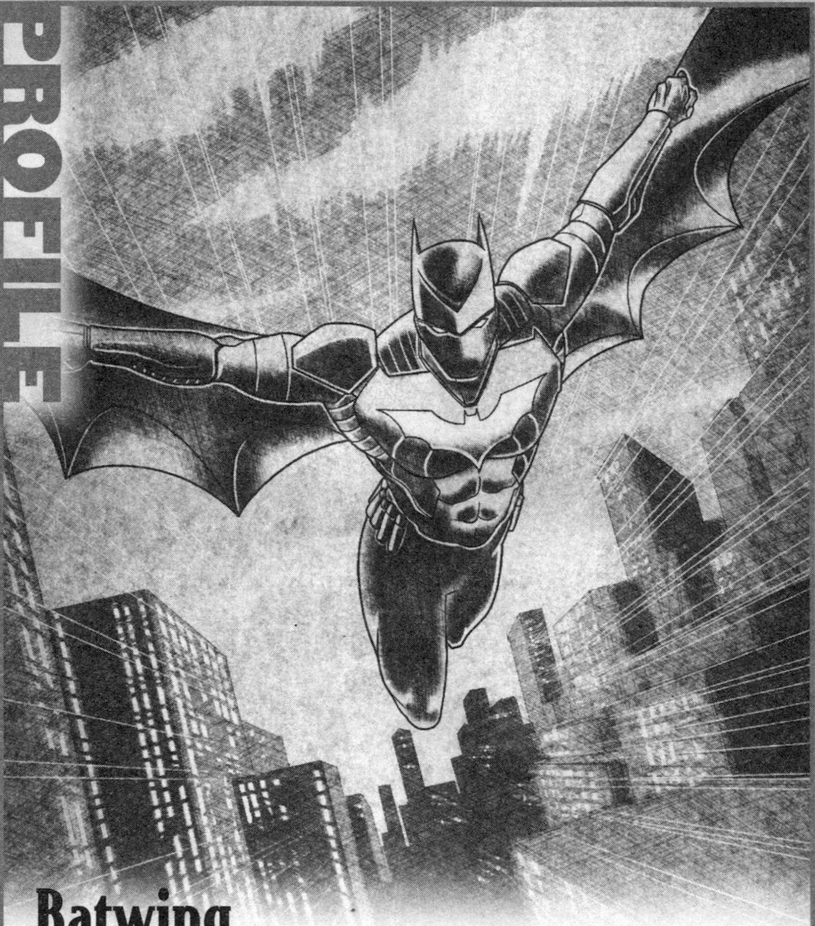
PROFILE

Batwing

Luke Fox's brilliant mind and skill as a mixed martial arts fighter attracted Batman's attention, and the Dark Knight soon asked Luke to take on the role of the crime fighter Batwing. Luke jumped at the chance. But after several missions, he decided to hang up the armored suit for a while. He began his own company, FoxTek, and later merged his efforts with those of his equally brilliant girlfriend, Barbara Gordon, creating Gordon Clean Energy.

The entire time, Qadir had no idea that the Super Hero Batgirl and his new friend, Barbara, were actually the same person.

Batgirl certainly needed all the help she could get. Burnside was full of new criminals she had never faced before. Batgirl even clashed with the artificial intelligence computer program she had created during her time using a wheelchair. The AI had taken on a life of its own and believed itself to be the true Barbara Gordon. The real Batgirl shut the program down, but Frankie Charles discovered Barbara's double identity in the process.

Frankie began offering her computer expertise to help guide Batgirl on her missions, whether Batgirl wanted her to or not. She quickly proved her worth during Batgirl's battle with a new villain called the Velvet Tiger. To save Batgirl's life, Frankie operated her Batcycle by remote control, crashing it into the Velvet Tiger. Batgirl quickly climbed aboard her cycle and was able to make a quick getaway unharmed.

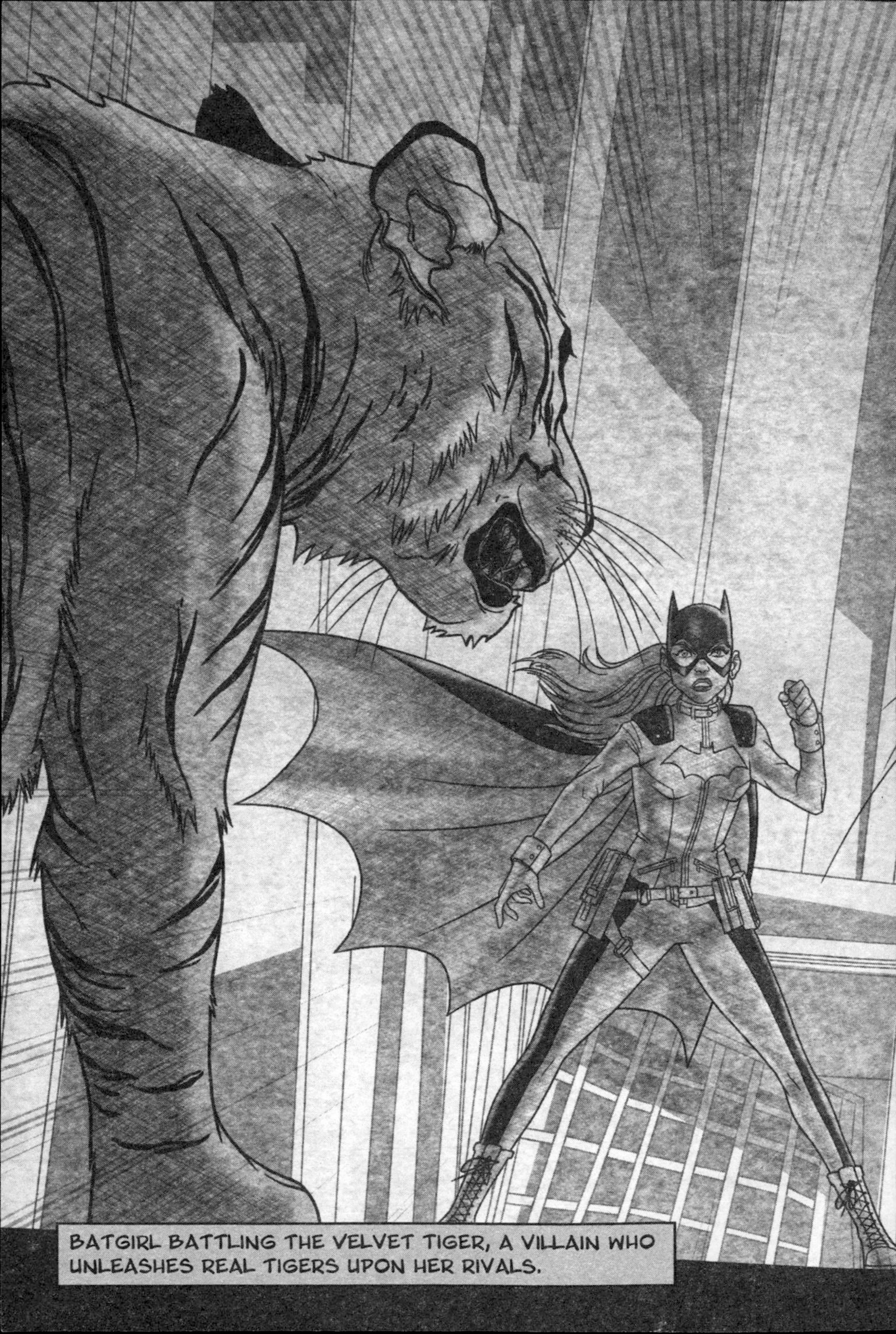

BATGIRL BATTLING THE VELVET TIGER, A VILLAIN WHO UNLEASHES REAL TIGERS UPON HER RIVALS.

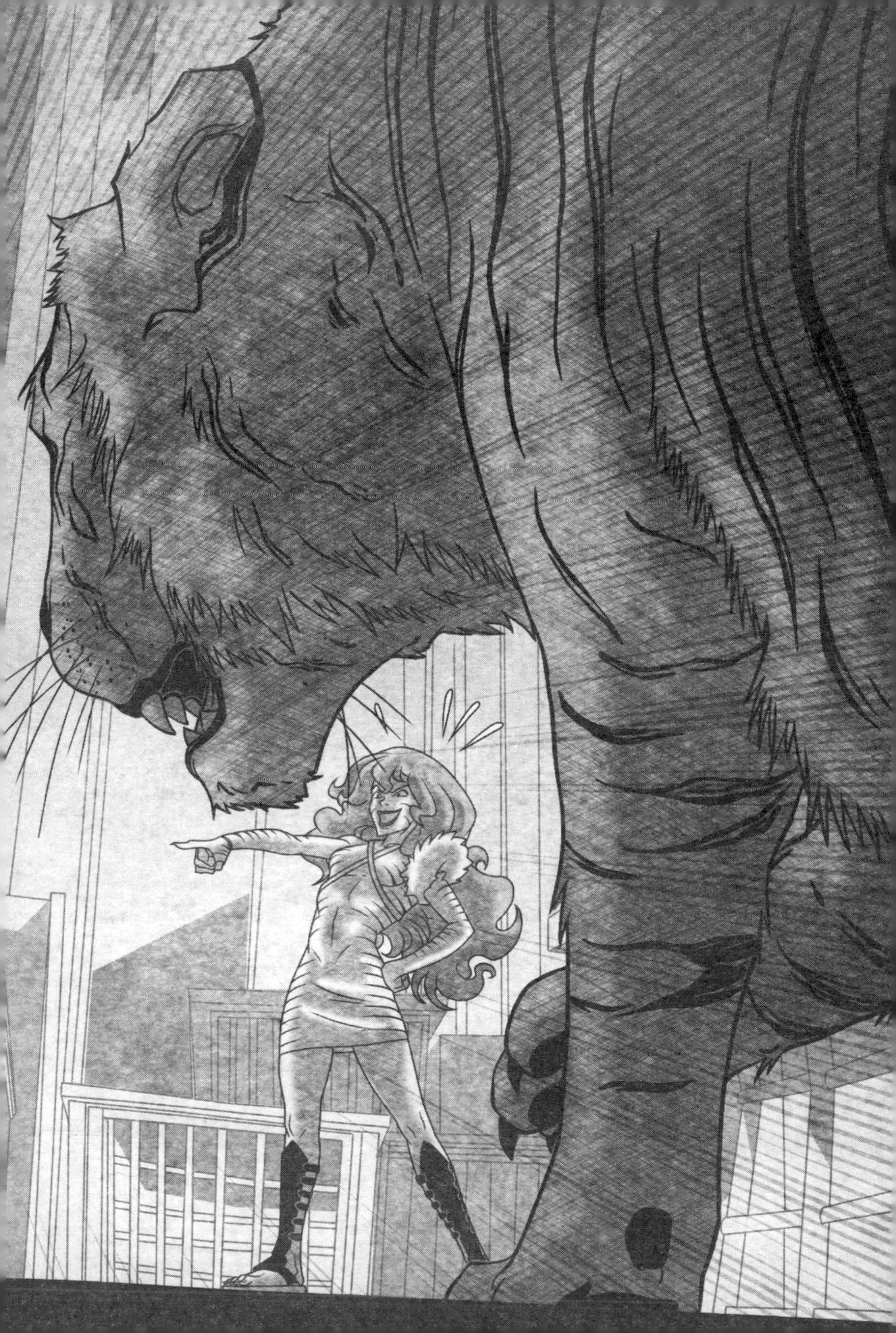

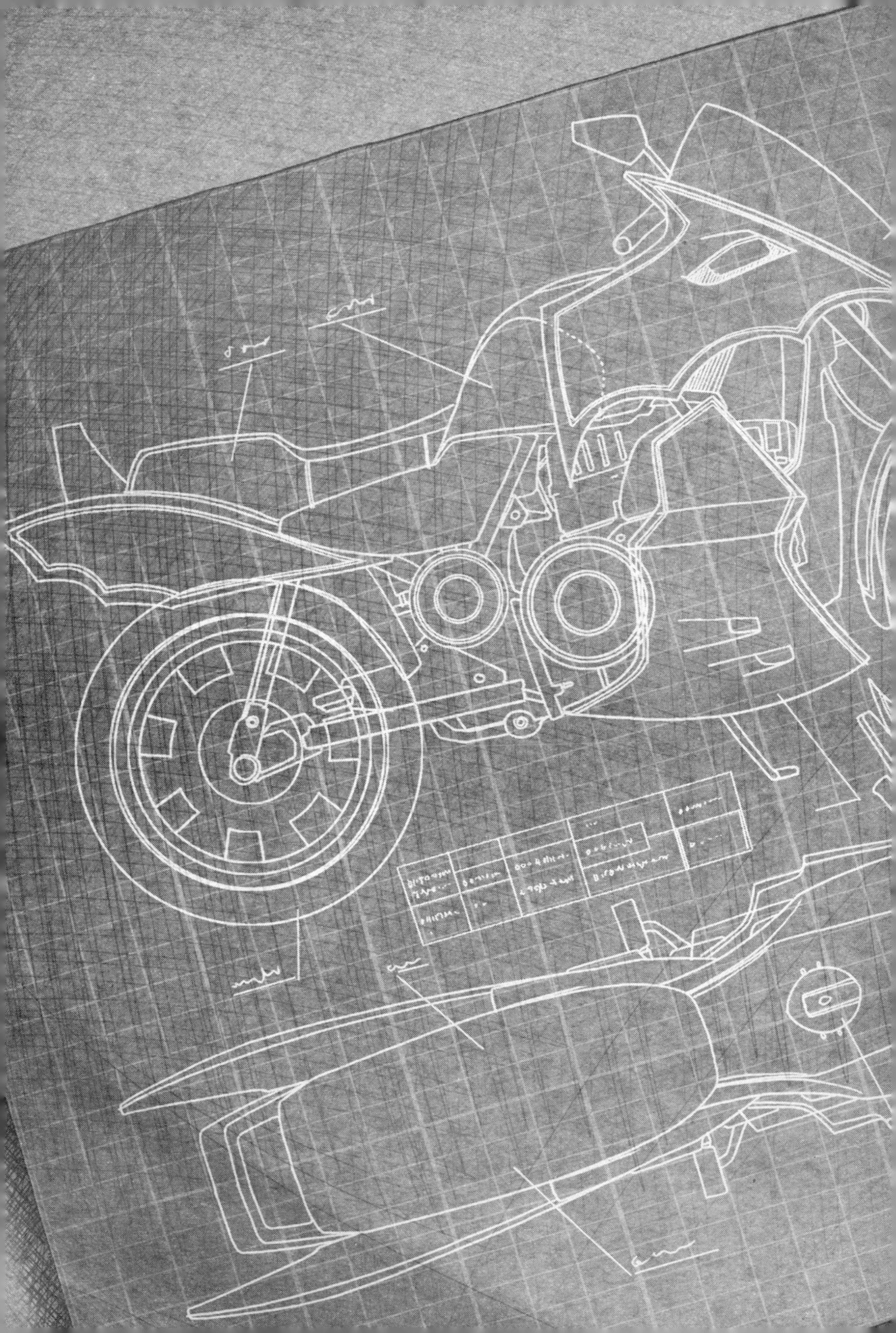

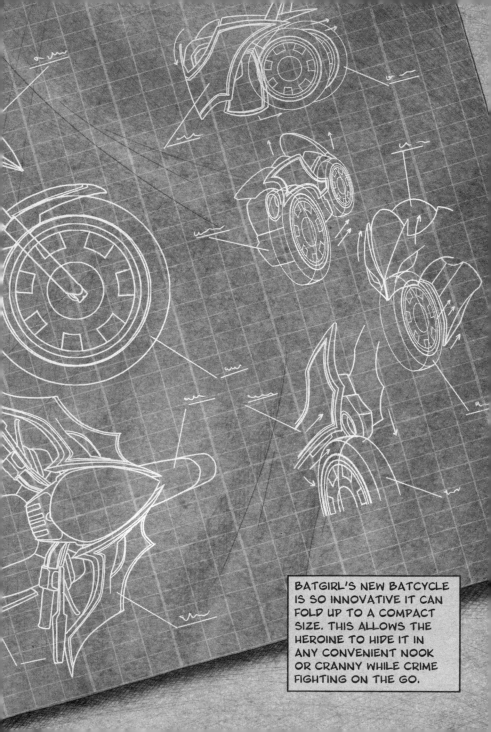

BATGIRL'S NEW BATCYCLE IS SO INNOVATIVE IT CAN FOLD UP TO A COMPACT SIZE. THIS ALLOWS THE HEROINE TO HIDE IT IN ANY CONVENIENT NOOK OR CRANNY WHILE CRIME FIGHTING ON THE GO.

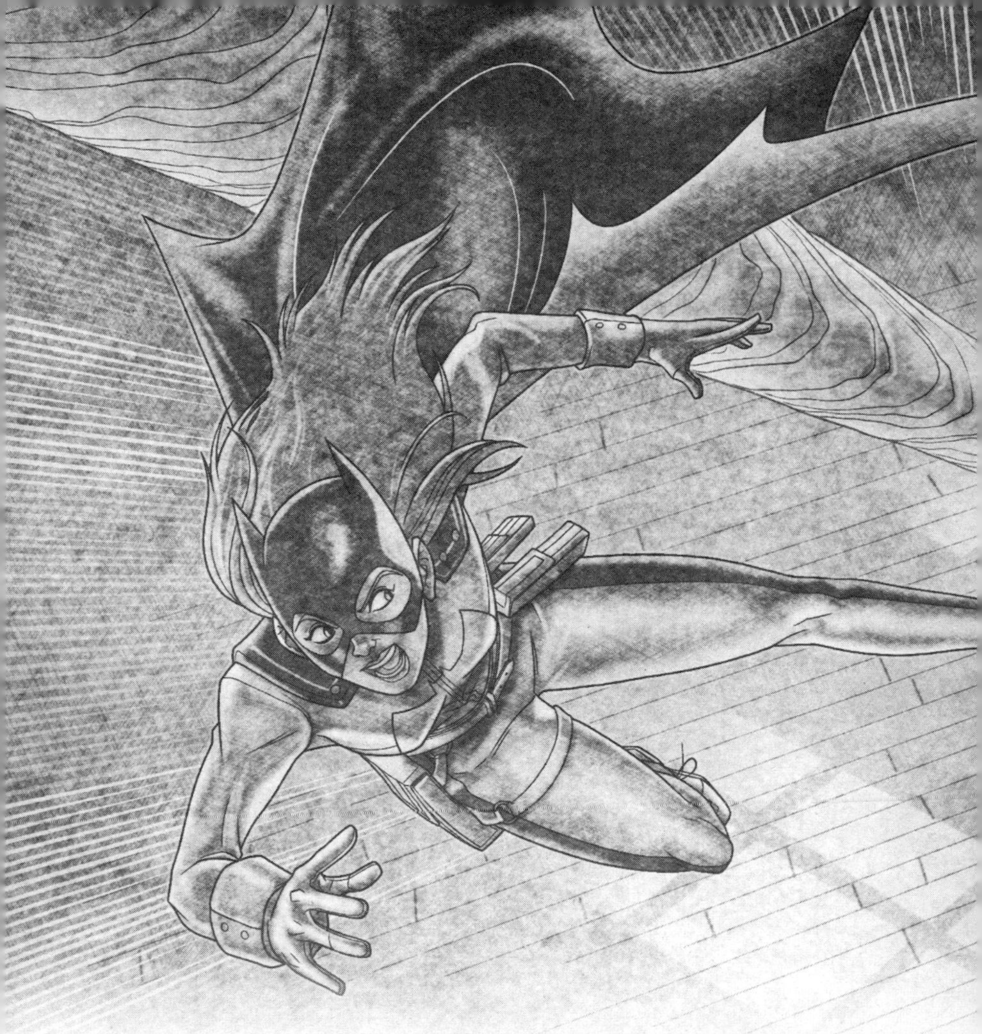

Frankie continued to butt into Batgirl's business until Barbara finally realized how helpful she was and allowed her to become her official partner, with the code name Operator.

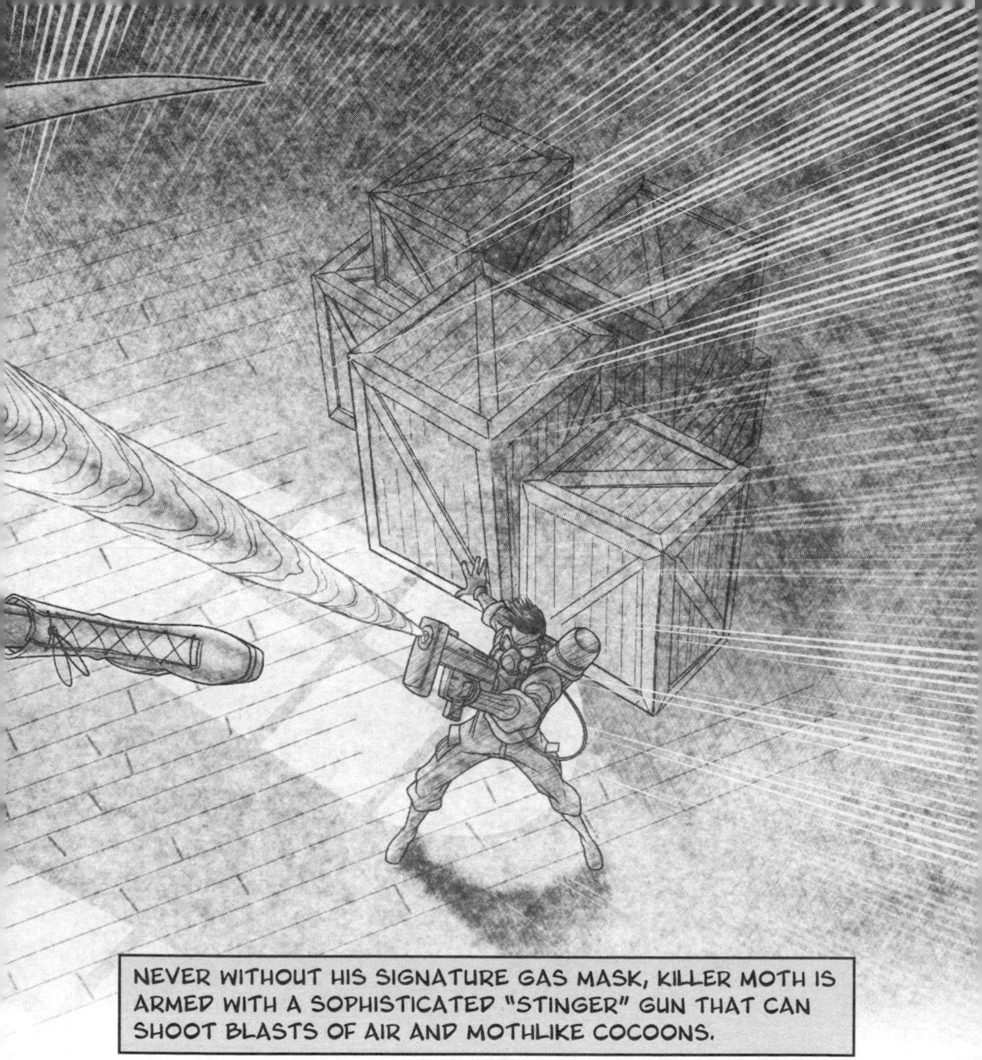
NEVER WITHOUT HIS SIGNATURE GAS MASK, KILLER MOTH IS ARMED WITH A SOPHISTICATED "STINGER" GUN THAT CAN SHOOT BLASTS OF AIR AND MOTHLIKE COCOONS.

Despite her busy life, Barbara soon made time for Luke Fox, the son of Wayne Enterprises CEO Lucius Fox. While he'd recently given up the life of a Super Hero to pursue a tech company called FoxTek, Luke

Fox had known Batgirl from his time as the armored vigilante Batwing. A quiet flirtation turned into a date or two, and Barbara soon found herself in a relationship with the sharp and handsome young man. Unlike the other men she had dated, Barbara was able to share both of her lives with Luke, and the two even joined forces as Super Heroes on rare occasion.

Burnside had become Batgirl's turf, and she protected it with the same dedication that Batman showed for the whole of Gotham City. But Batgirl's greatest challenge in her new home came when a villain called the Fugue began to literally haunt her dreams. Able to shift the memories of anyone he chooses, the Fugue held an old grudge against Barbara Gordon and wanted nothing more than to frame her for the destruction of the borough she so loved. To accomplish that, he united Batgirl's latest enemies, including Velvet Tiger and Killer Moth. The Fugue planned to lure the citizens of Burnside to the

Burnside Bridge and then detonate a clean energy device Barbara Gordon and Luke Fox had been developing.

With the help of many of her friends, including Black Canary and the Operator, Batgirl stopped the Fugue, overcoming his fake memories with her own wit and expert fighting skills. Barbara Gordon was free to return to her life, knowing she had saved the citizens of her newly adopted home.

Gotham City is a dark place for anyone to live. But Barbara Gordon has paved her own path and found a light to help illuminate the shadows. She now runs Gordon Clean Energy with her partner and boyfriend, Luke Fox. The two are currently developing a way to use renewable energy to help power Gotham

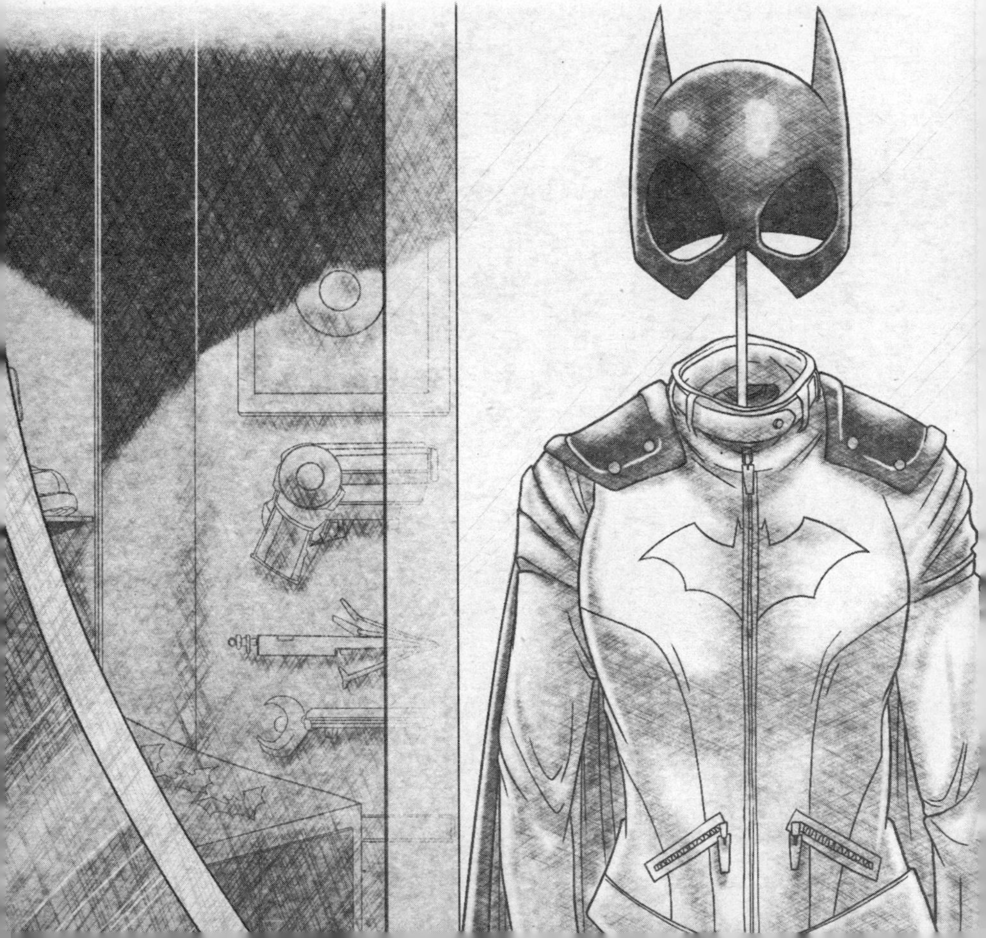

City. Barbara has even hired a staff composed of her friends, including Frankie, Alysia, and Qadir.

Underneath Barbara's new business headquarters is a basement bunker designed by Frankie and accessible only to the two of them. In the basement is a sealed vault that hides a motorcycle, a costume,

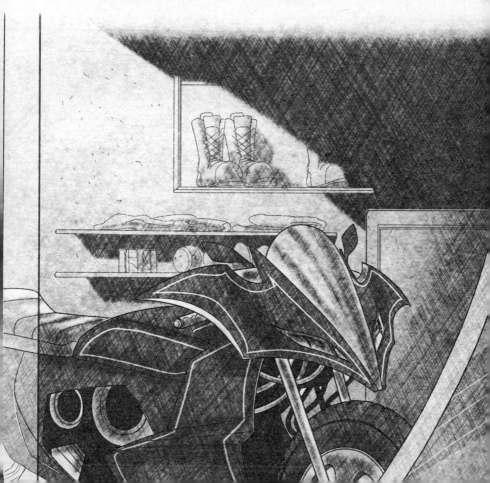

and an entire host of gadgets, waiting for night to once again fall on the borough of Burnside. Because night is when the real Barbara Gordon comes out to play. Night in Burnside belongs to Batgirl.

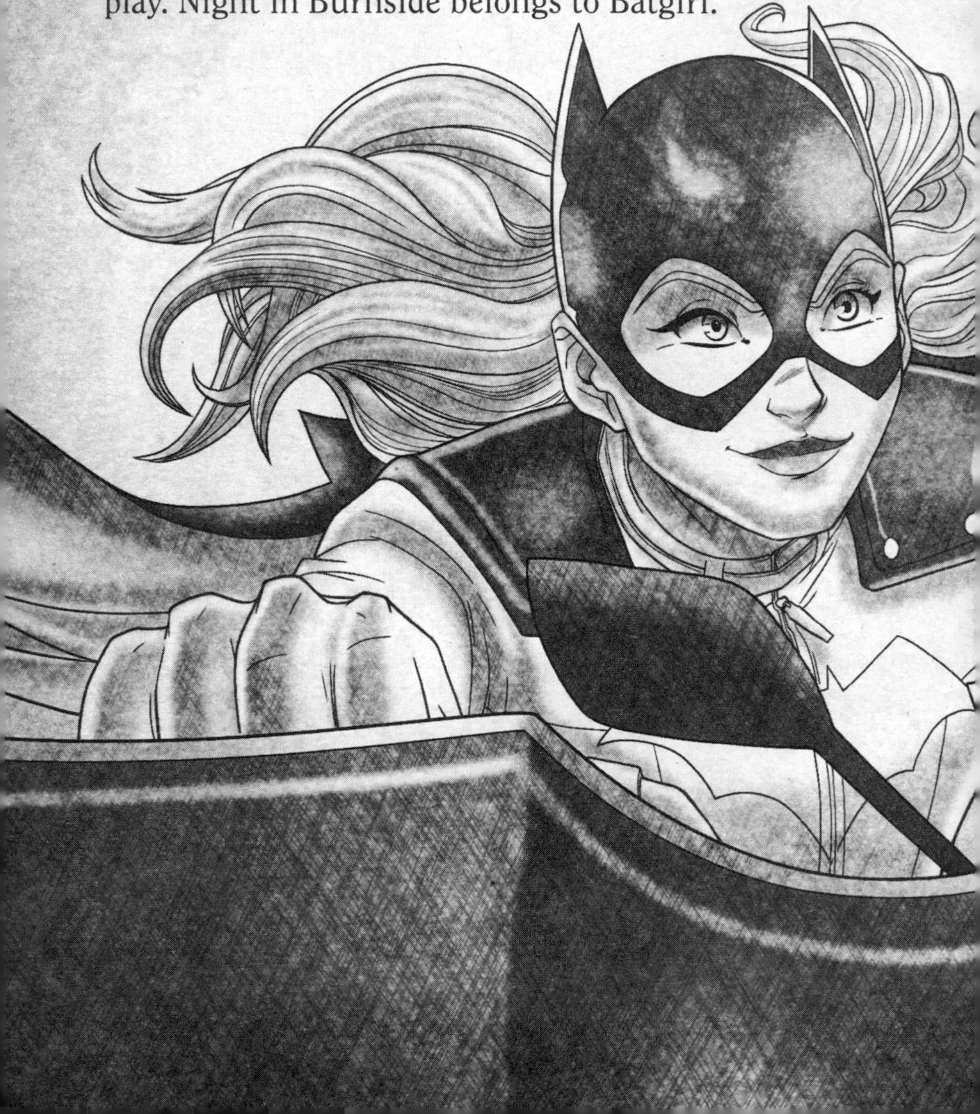

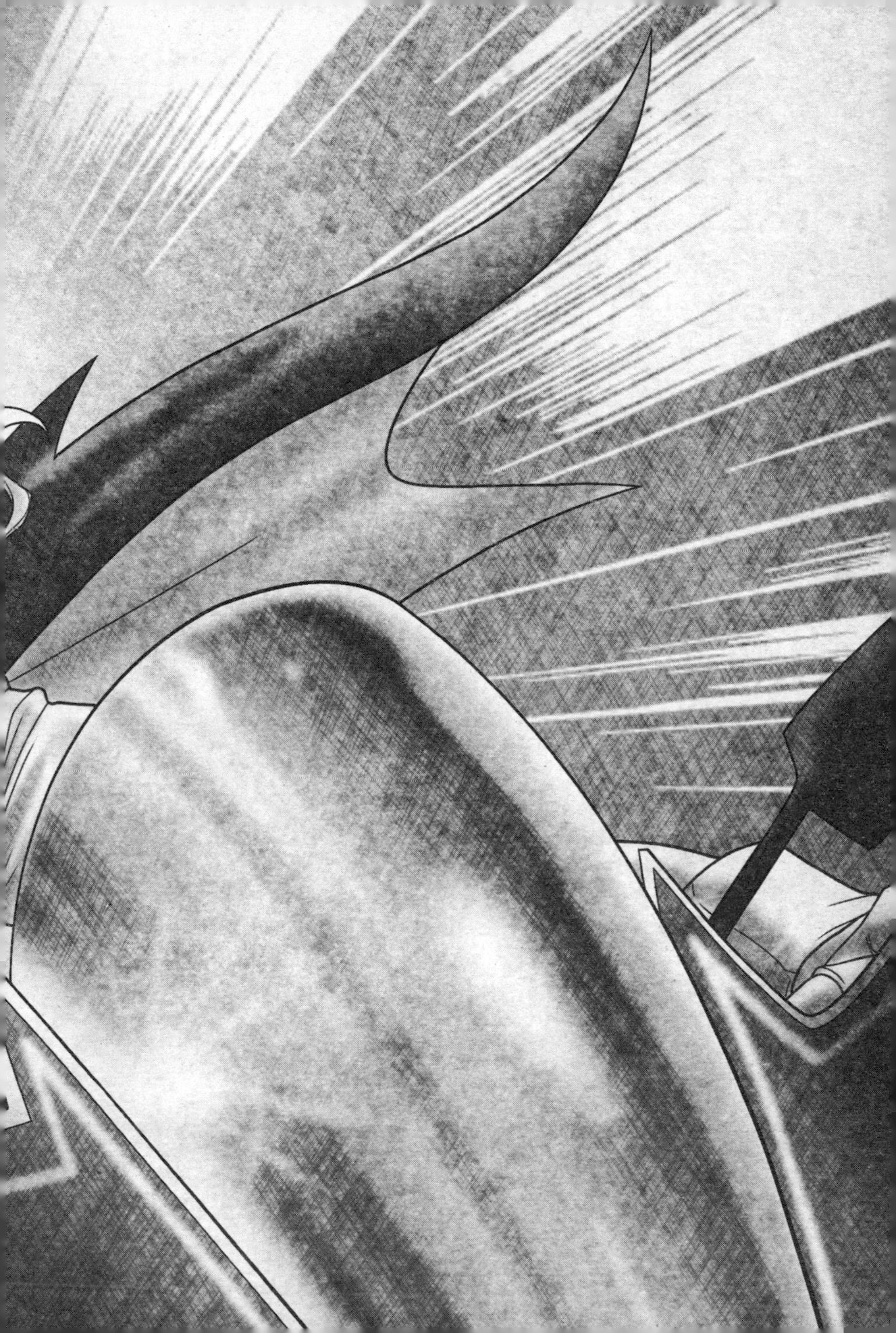

Fast Facts

- Batgirl is the daughter of Gotham City Police Commissioner James Gordon and his estranged wife, Barbara Kean Gordon.

- The first super-villain Batgirl ever fought was a cult leader named Harry X.

- Batgirl has worn three official costumes over the years, not including the prototype Batsuit she wore to battle Harry X.

- Batgirl uses a Batcycle, sometimes called the Batgirl Cycle, to get around Gotham City.

- Barbara Gordon's closest friends include former roommate Alysia Yeoh, current roommate Frankie Charles, and Birds of Prey teammate Black Canary.

Batgirl was shot and paralyzed by the Joker during his plot to drive her father insane.

Batgirl expected Batman to give her a lecture after the Joker defeated her. Instead, the Caped Crusader showed a rare glimpse of his tender side and simply held her hand in support.

Batgirl is only one of the many partners to officially work with Batman. Others include Nightwing, Red Hood, Red Robin, and Robin.

The entire inner Batman family knows Barbara's secret identity, including Bruce Wayne's butler, Alfred Pennyworth. Batgirl knows their alter egos as well.

- Barbara's little brother, James Gordon Jr., has repeatedly tried to defeat her, proving himself one of her greatest enemies.

- Batgirl is a founding member of the Birds of Prey, alongside Black Canary and Starling.

- The second Robin, Jason Todd, grew up to become the Red Hood. He maintains a crush on Batgirl.

- The artificial intelligence program Barbara Gordon created while paralyzed nearly destroyed Burnside when plotting its revenge against Batgirl.

- Batgirl's memory is so accurate that she can recall the events of a previous day as if reliving them.

Batgirl once briefly served in a strike force arm of the Justice League called the Justice League United.

Both Knightfall and the Fugue have recruited other villains to team up and battle Batgirl. The heroine only survived the conflicts with help from her own Super Hero allies.

Barbara Gordon's current boyfriend is Luke Fox, the second hero to adopt the name of Batwing. Together, they run the start-up company called Gordon Clean Energy.

Glossary

allegiance: Loyalty to a person, group, or cause.

arsenal: A collection of weapons.

artificial intelligence: The capability of a machine to imitate intelligent human behavior.

borough: A village, town, or part of a large city.

chronology: A list of events in the order of when they happened.

corrupt: Dishonest or immoral.

cowl: A hood. In Batgirl's case, it is the mask part of her costume.

criminology: The study of crime and criminals.

eidetic: Able to recall memories with vivid accuracy and detail, as if they are actually visible.

judo: A sport developed in Japan in which opponents attempt to throw each other through the use of quick movements and leverage.

pyromaniac: A person with an irresistible impulse to start fires.

paralyze: To make a person or animal unable to move or to feel all or part of the body.

rogue: Isolated or uncontrollable, not part of a team.

telekinetic: Able to make objects move without making contact with them.

vigilante: A person who is not a member of law enforcement but pursues and punishes criminals.

[redacted]

BACKSTORIES™

Uncover the epic histories of your favorite characters!

BACKSTORIES
DC COMICS
SUPERMAN
THE MAN OF TOMORROW
SCHOLASTIC

BACKSTORIES
DC COMICS
SUPERGIRL
DAUGHTER OF KRYPTON
SCHOLASTIC

BACKSTORIES
DC COMICS
BATMAN
GOTHAM CITY'S GUARDIAN
SCHOLASTIC

BACKSTORIES
DC COMICS
WONDER WOMAN
AMAZON WARRIOR
SCHOLASTIC

BACKSTORIES
DC COMICS
HARLEY QUINN
WILD CARD
SCHOLASTIC

Read them all!